"It's a wonderful book! This is as good a self-help book as I have ever read. Ira brings his early life experiences that helped him—and then turns it into a terrific work that will help you. An important book—a page turner too!"

—LARRY KING Formerly, CNN's "Larry King Live"

Ensure Your Cure in Psychotherapy

The Art & Science
of Patients' Success

Ira Schwartz, Ph.D.

outskirts
press

Note: A cure in psychotherapy is not finite as in some medical conditions. For example, it's clearly a cure when an x-ray reveals the absence of a germ that previously was present and was treated. For the purposes of this book, the term "cure" is defined by Sigmund Freud's description of the aim of treatment:

"Our aim will not be to rub off every peculiarity of human character... The business of the analysis is to secure the best possible psychological conditions for the function of the ego; with that it has discharged its task."

Sigmund Freud, "Analysis Terminable and Interminable" (1937), *Standard Edition of the Complete Works of Sigmund Freud*, 23, p. 250.

Table of Contents

Introduction

A Fateful Day

DECEMBER 17, 1947 was a sunny winter day, perfect for a game of punchball. At 12-years old, I was a good student, an athlete, and had many friends. So, at lunchtime, I ran down the stairs of Brooklyn's Seth Low Junior High School and jogged home, eager to gulp down a sandwich and milk before sprinting back to Seth Low Park to meet my pals.

I arrived at 1619 West 12ᵗʰ Street, left the sunny world, and entered my home only to be startled upon seeing Leo, my 28-year-old brother, leaning on the upstairs railing. I wondered, "What's he doing here at lunchtime? Something's not right." "He and Dad are business partners, always together at work." Cautiously, I muttered, "Hi."

Leo replied, "Dad died!" I felt stunned and staggered up the stairs. Upon reaching the landing, Leo stammered: "Dad… fell down the stairs…. No… he killed himself…. He hung himself." Then, I felt weird.

I was oppressed by that feeling for 16 years, until I found psychotherapy, which slowly relieved my despair, humiliation, and terror. It helped me recover from the blow of my father's suicide and accomplish things my 12-year-old self never knew were possible.

Why Did He Do It?

There's never an easy answer to a suicide. Perhaps his problem began when his 21-year-old sister and he, a six-year-old orphan, migrated in 1901 to New York from Hungary. It appears that early hardships twisted his nature into a brutal man, yet he apparently became helpless when facing the bankruptcy of his business, which occurred shortly before he committed suicide.

His Inner Viciousness Had Been Percolating

Prior to his suicide, his inner viciousness boiled over, and on several occasions, he beat me. Before telling you how, please realize that therapy helped me overcome those early traumas, and I am recounting these stories to help other people realize they can find relief through treatment too.

My father first beat me when I was four-years old. He told me to kiss my sister, after she had her tonsils removed, but I didn't want to. I defied him. Without warning, he started swinging. Frightened, I thought, "One more smack and that's what death is." At four, death seemed an unknowable painful something. Thankfully, he stopped.

Then, at age nine, while sitting at my desk, doing homework, I heard him talking angrily on the telephone in another room. Next, I heard his heavy, scary footsteps. I froze as the thumping of his shoes came closer and closer, from the hallway, to my doorway, and into my room. Finally, his huge frame straddled me. Without a word, he raised his former prizefighter's hand and from overhead delivered a slap to my face that knocked me off my chair.

While on the floor—my face stinging, feeling shocked and disgraced—I looked up at him, terrified. But my fright eased: He looked self-satisfied and turned, marched out, and never uttered a word.

What was my offense? I smoked a cigarette. In fact, it barely touched my lips, which, for the moment, made me feel like a big man—after all, my father previously beat me into feeling like a "little guy." Actually, smoking was not my thing—I wanted to be an athlete.

Shortly after that series of smacks, a feeling of dread overtook me, which surfaced in a terrifying nightmare of a hand coming out of the ceiling light and in a frightening attack of asthma that caused me to gasp for breath.

"Your Dad"

When I was ten, and my father was in Europe on a business trip for six months, I wrote a letter to him. Some parts of his return letter—written around 1945, shortly after World War II ended—reveal more about his nature and are shown below. (See Appendix A for a typed copy of his full letter and Appendix B for a photocopy of his handwritten letter.)

> Dear Ira was very glad to hear from you I think you that you care for me better ~~I~~ than the rest of family outside of Mother & Lillian [my oldest sister; I am the youngest of five siblings] as they have written but the rest well they are all Big sh ts Well to prove to you that ~~a~~ I appreciate the letter you have written whatever bad you have done since I went away I will forget, But Lord pitty you if you make any wrong moves from now on … Biggest of all is our family. I did not do any business in Italy as yet but I will and & I will make arrangements before I get through that you & Donald & Wallace [Leo's sons] & rest of my boys will have something to look forward to if you are smart enough…. I do hope that you don't give Mother & Janice [my sister] no trouble …. Give My regard to all
>
> Your Dad

So, because I wrote to him, he forgave me for any *future wrong-doings I might commit*. Wasn't that decent of him? Considering I was an "A" student, well-behaved, and athletic, he must have been relieved not to have the job, once again, of beating me to a pulp. In all his kindness, he gave me a temporary pass and hoped the "lord would pity" me, in case… In case of what? In case I didn't achieve A's on all my tests? Or, perhaps, I wore the wrong tie to school?

His warnings and unfounded threats left me feeling anxious and distressed. His letter lacked any interest in how I was doing, and he never mentioned his not having written to me or his family. Six months was a long time to be apart in the years before Skype, email, and instant messaging. His emotional detachment and lack of interest in me lowered my self-esteem. He caused me to doubt myself by writing, "You will have something to look forward to *if you are smart enough*." How is that for arrogance from a father towards his own son? That's especially so, if *his grammar* is compared to my having been in the top class in my grade, which he never acknowledged.

As a kid, I only wanted to do right by my family, do my chores, do well in school, have friends, and play sports. My father, in response and without cause, repeatedly terrorized me, yet *suggested* he loved me by signing his letter, "Your Dad," without including an affectionate closing—"Love." The only thing that was clear, in this mish mash of confusion, was his potential to lash out at me. I must have been his favorite, being the only one of five children he tore into.

Although I did derive a feeling of physical security, based on the comforts of having food and a home, I was without a loving emotional involvement from family. Inevitably, being physically cared for became intertwined with feeling terrorized. My father's suicide brought this mixed contradiction of caring and fear to a boil, a swirling knotted mess of psychological distress that only psychotherapy could unravel, soothe, and resolve. That overall experience, in part, led me to write *Ensure...* so others might use therapy effectively.

Moving Forward

After my father's suicide, I stumbled through life, but gained some stability by immersing myself in basketball, friendships, and studies. However, I was terrified *constantly* that people would discover that my father killed himself and think something was wrong with me, because I was the son of a man who committed suicide. My family, never emotionally expressive, withdrew into themselves and left me to my own wits while feeling alone.

Psychotherapy helped me to overcome those hardships and effectively build a happy, successful life. My dismal childhood is presented not as an appeal for sympathy, but rather in the hope you'll see the power in psychotherapy, when used effectively, in the light of how it helped me transform myself. If you can do that, then my story is priceless: Treatment enabled me to turn my entire life around.

I learned how to get the most out of each therapy session. I'm sharing those techniques to help you ensure your cure and become free to direct your life by choice. If you need further proof of the benefits of psychotherapy, here's what it enabled me to accomplish:

I began therapy a few years after receiving my bachelor's degree from Hunter College. Later on, I became the first health counselor in New York City's More Effective Schools program, helping poverty-stricken children overcome health problems.

My interest in health expanded into psychology: Ph.D. degree, Hofstra University, school and clinical psychology; since 1972, private practice, Brooklyn, NY; and, consultant to several hospitals and schools. I am the author of three books: *Your Hotspots...* (Athelia Henrietta Press, 2001); *Ensure* (Outskirts, 2016); and *On Striving with Finesse* (not yet published). Three of my papers were published in the *American Journal of Forensic Psychology*, and, my "Family Advice" column ran weekly in *The Brooklyn Times*.

My wife is a watercolorist, and I am a woodcarver. We live and play tennis in Brooklyn, New York and Delray Beach, Florida.

There isn't any way that the frightened boy I was could become the man I am other than through psychotherapy. It worked for me, and it can work for you, too. Just read *Ensure* and discover all you need to know and do.

ONE

Why Do Some People Need Psychotherapy?

OUR EMOTIONS RUN deep. Consider some everyday sayings: "She's the love of my life"; "He makes me so mad, sometimes I want to kill him"; "I'd go to the end of the earth for him"; "She's my one and only"; "I swear, you'll give me a heart attack." Many a truth is said in sayings.

So, when frustrated, some people's emotions become tangled, mixed, confused, or discouraged and wear on them, which can cause colitis, ulcers... or, nightmares, depression, anxiety... Emotional disorders seem to know no bounds: sometimes we are aware of them, but at other times, they are embedded deep within ourselves, making them hard for us to recognize and resolve.

For example, a man unknowingly could be harboring rage, or anger, from deep within, which sometimes leads to his flaring up. He is unable to see that raging is a mishandling of his emotions, because it has become a part of who he is, which is a problem for him and those around. He needs the special methods of psychotherapy, whether he agrees or not, for help in becoming aware of what causes him to flare up, which can lead to his developing new and effective ways to handle himself.

Obviously, you're a step ahead of the man in that example—you're busy reading a book on how to achieve a cure. However, whatever your problem may be, psychotherapy can help you overcome it providing you *commit to adjusting to its special methods.* That's where *Ensure* comes into play.

Symptoms of a Larger Problem

As previously noted, sometimes emotional disorders appear as physical illnesses. When patients complain about aches and pains, fatigue, irritability, depression, or anxiety, their physicians usually take a history and run tests. If no physical disorder is uncovered, their physicians might suspect that emotional or psychological issues are the cause, which are often sensitive matters. Therefore, physicians initially may try to ease patients directly—by prescribing medication or being emotionally supportive. Then they wait and see. Often, time is a great healer. For those patients who are relieved, "All's well that ends well."

However, if a patient's stress persists in causing disturbing feelings, thoughts, or physical problems, his or her plight can worsen. When stress becomes chronic, it can surface in the mind (the *psyche*) and result in a mental disorder, such as anxiety, depression, or mood swings. In other cases, ongoing stress can convert into the body (*soma*), and cause relatively minor physical illnesses, such as headaches and stomach distress, or severe disorders, such as ulcers or colitis, as noted previously.

When stress affects the mind and the body as well, the illness is termed *psychosomatic*. (Of course, psychosomatic pertains to a real physical illness but is sometimes misconstrued to be imaginary.) Should physicians sense that their patients' distress is mounting, they refer them to psychotherapists. Alternatively, many patients who suffer from ongoing physical or emotional problems seek therapy on their own.

Emotions vs. Logic

If a person has discord in a relationship, but resolves it by taking some reasonable or *logical* action—say, marriage, having a child, reaching an agreement, or buying a house—then life becomes beautiful once again for him or her. It follows, for such a fortunate person, there would be no frustration, no stress, no emotional disorder, and no psychotherapy.

However, sometimes distress in a relationship, or from another situation, remains unresolved, or the causes of a person's distress are undetermined. Then, unruly and unorganized emotions, such as frustration, anger, depression…, build-up within an individual. If pent-up emotions cause sustained inner pressure, a person's mind and body will suffer from wear and tear. If no logical intervention relieves the emotional distress, then the *special methods of psychotherapy* are sought, to effectively reach and resolve the sources of emotional distress.

Therefore, first logical interventions are attempted, and if no success, then psychotherapy is pursued. The latter's unique methods are geared to reach the emotions. In short, *the single most important task for a patient is to learn how to use psychotherapy's special methods to become* **cooperative** *with her therapist in reaching the emotions.* Conversely, for a therapist to be effective, he or she must have a patient's full cooperation.

Some Additional Reasons to Develop Cooperativeness

It is difficult to overcome emotional problems, in part, because logic does not reach or relieve embroiled emotions that are rooted in the *unconscious,* a region of the mind harboring thoughts, feelings, and memories blocked out of our awareness. If logic could do the job, we could readily eliminate obesity, sexually transmitted diseases, bad decisions…, and we could write a book entitled, *Psychological Problems Eliminated by Using Logic.*

The major reason logic usually does not reach and overcome our troubled emotions follows: logic uses the *rules* of our language, namely, *syntax;* in contrast, the emotions are *feelings,* which are *subjective*—they don't abide by rules or logic. For example, when two people fall in love, but they are unlikely candidates for each other, sometimes we hear interested parties complain, "They are a bad match."

However, there is the saying, "Love is blind," so those lovers' emotions might cause a blindness that won't let them see the logic apparent to their friends and relatives.

Presumably, if relentless desires did in fact yield to logic, emotional sufferers, again, wouldn't require therapy. If those desires, lodged in our unconscious minds, understood and obeyed our logic, we could order our nightmares to disappear and replace them with good dreams only. Emotions can hold on as tenaciously as a pit bull does. They can preserve something or someone, from the past or in the present, in reality or in memory. However, psychotherapy's translators, therapists, use a special method that can help relieve emotional distress.

With Blinders on, We Commit Follies

Those people whose hidden follies dictate the direction of their lives ultimately become snagged in emotional and other problems. In a sense, they wear *emotional blinders,* which allow only their folly to see what the folly wants to see. The book *Yiddish Wisdom* quotes the saying, handed down from the ages, that, "He who is aware of his folly is wise."[1]

For instance, a man opened a store in Brooklyn that sold only things colored fuchsia. He went out of business in a few years. His blinders prevented him from perceiving that not everyone loves fuchsia, and that three out of five retail stores fail within the first five years of opening. His folly? A false belief: "Because I love fuchsia, everyone will love fuchsia."

Removing Your Blinders

In considering the familiar saying, "Love is blind," we can infer *emotional blindness,* or the inability to see flaws in loved ones or in oneself. Individuals hampered by emotional blindness suffer from stress in relationships and, as described previously, that can lead to physical or emotional disorders.

Some people repeatedly try to cope with the troublesome flaws in themselves or others with whom they are emotionally involved, but do so ineffectively. In those cases, even when flaws are discovered, many people are unable to see and handle things differently, in order to reshape their relationships and reduce stress.

A psychotherapist has a better perspective, much like a carriage horse and its driver. The carriage horse wears blinders, so its view of the world is limited. The driver, on the other hand, is able to direct the horse to a better path, because she has a wider view from her seat on the carriage and can see obstacles that the horse would miss.

Psychotherapists are able to recognize patients' blinders. Each patient is an individual, yet in my own practice, I frequently encounter patients caught up in this plight. For example, one man, in an initial consultation, said he was going to take substantial time off from his job because he felt stressed by it. I suggested he not make any major decisions until we were able to talk further, sensing he was unable to "see" (due to his blinders) that a temporary withdrawal from his perceived source of stress indicated signs of a serious avoidance problem.

Fortunately, he complied: huge blinders blocked his seeing a long-standing avoidance problem, which prevented him from achieving fulfillment in his career and relationships. During the course of his psychotherapy, he was able to diminish stress by developing the capacity to work constructively in his profession and other endeavors.

Follies are usually entrenched in emotional disorders, a complication that blocks effective communication between the intellect and the emotions. When that is the situation, those people are unable to modify their own emotional disorders. In a sense, they need translators—again, therapists—to help them. Therapists help people reach their emotions and then tactfully assist them to become aware of their follies. Eventually, most patients appreciate the benefits derived from that enlightenment.

Pressure from Stress

Stress is caused by a person's inner psychological problems that prevent the effective handling of relationships or change. As stress builds up, mental and psychosomatic disorders can develop. Furthermore, ineffective coping skills lead to frustration, feeling overwhelmed, and regression to employing problematical ways of relating, such as pouting after having been corrected. Those ineffective methods have their roots in childhood. Over time, the use of futile ways of relating increases emotional distress.

Stress can result from *positive or negative changes*, such as either obtaining or losing a job. One physician studied stress induced by changes in life circumstances and found that death of a spouse, divorce, and separation were the top three stress factors, in that order. Note that each of those factors, on a rather long and diversified list, concerned relationships.[2]

The effects of relationship problems are even more far-reaching. Yes, love can be blind, but so can other emotions as well—such as anger. At the extreme, consider this eye-opener concerning the importance of being effective in relationships: nearly half of the over 20,000 homicide victims reported in 1996 in the U.S. were related to or acquainted with their killers.[3] Should the killers' rage turn inward, the perpetrator becomes the victim, by committing suicide or developing a psychological or physical disorder.

Troubled Relationships

Focusing on your relationships in therapy is of ultimate importance. That issue is so significant that Lester Luborsky and his colleagues developed a questionnaire, the Core Conflictual Relationship Theme (CCRT), to evaluate how people relate to each other. You might consider discussing with your therapist the following topics from the CCRT:

- The desires you have expressed to your partner.
- What he or she said in return.

- The emotions and actions you expressed or took.
- Relate the details: who, what, when, and where of the scenario.[4]

With your therapist's assistance, analyze your relationship dialogues—the "he said, she said" exchanges regarding people in your life. That analysis can lead to mental and physical health. Our minds, our bodies, our well-being, and our lives depend on the intricacies of what we say to each other. Be as specific as shown above in the CCRT. Enable your therapist to use his or her "third ear," as Theodore Reik put it, to understand and help analyze your dialogues and assist you in improving or restoring your relationships and your health.

Empathy, the Essence of A Healthy Relationship

Empathy, the ability to understand another person and express that understanding to him or her, is the mainstay of relationships. Whether you agree or disagree with people, you can still show you understand their point of view. When you show empathy, people feel more comfortable. Try it—in the next conversation, restate the essence of what your companion said.

Carl Rogers based his entire treatment on empathy. His specific technique, termed *reflection,* consists of merely restating the essence of what another person says, the general idea of it, which is the ultimate in empathy.

Empathy helps reach a person blinded by his or her emotions. Hence, the old edict: "Never reason with an angry person." Since logic (reason) and emotions (feelings) "speak different languages," logic won't be understood or heard by an angry (or emotionally upset) person. It's clear: When their emotions are inflamed, people become blind to logic, so using logic at that time only irritates the person's anger. Usually it is better to empathize with their feelings rather than attempt to reason with or talk them out of being furious. An example of what to say might be, "Apparently, you are quite furious with …"

You might be best, for the time being, to leave it at that, without adding any "buts," "howevers," or "maybes." After empathizing with them, wait and see how they react. Perhaps, letting them cool off for a while will work.

The most important way in which therapists relate is by being empathetic. Don't think they are being repetitive when they frequently say "I understand." They mean it; if they didn't, they would ask for your clarification. Pay attention to your therapist's use of it, and then maximize your benefit by using the trust it generates as a springboard for your further opening up.

While your therapist makes an effort to understand what you are saying, make sure you understand her or him as well. Then, take it a step further—become successful in *all* spheres of life by using therapy to develop your capacity to be empathetic in general.

Couples who are empathetic enjoy happy relationships; those who are not, suffer from relationship discord. For their own benefit, self-absorbed patients should seriously consider using their therapy to develop a sincere interest in other people, and a good place to start is with being empathetic. In doing so, more than likely, they will feel gratified, while also becoming an even more important person to others. That brings us to the next chapter, in which you will discover the rock-solid scientific basis of psychotherapy.

REFERENCES – ONE

1. *Yiddish Wisdom,* (San Francisco: Chronicle Books, 1996), p. 52.

2. Thomas J. Holmes, "The Stress of Adjusting to Change," *The New York Times,* June 10, 1973, quoted in *Comprehensive Textbook of Psychiatry,* II, 2nd ed., ed. A.M. Freeman, et al., Linn, "Clinical Manifestations of Psychiatric Disorders" (Baltimore: Williams & Wilkins, 1975), p. 785.

3. Charles Patrick Ewing, *Fatal Families: The Dynamics of Intrafamilial Homicide* (California: Sage Publications, 1997).

4. Lester Luborsky et al, (1995). "A Comparison of Core Conflictual Relationship Themes Before Psychotherapy and During Early Sessions," *Journal of Consulting and Clinical Psychology,* Vol. 63, No. 1, 145-148.

TWO

The Facts About Therapy

Proof Positive

PERHAPS YOU'RE STILL not convinced—even after having read the introduction to *Ensure*—that through therapy you too can fulfill your desire for a cure. Hopefully, the following results from Jonathan Shedler's major research will help. In 2010, he reviewed 792 studies on the outcomes of psychotherapy and then compared the effectiveness of *psychodynamic psychotherapy* (depth therapy, the type covered in *Ensure*) to all other treatments.

He found the psychodynamic method, which emphasizes an analysis of the psychological forces underlying behavior and emotions, *to be more effective than all other therapies* and *three times more effective than drug therapy*.[1] (Of course, certain conditions, such as schizophrenia, usually require the use of pharmacotherapy, often in conjunction with psychotherapy.) Shedler's meta-analysis is irrefutable and has had a powerful effect on how therapists treat patients.

The Basic Psychotherapy Technique Led to A Nobel Prize

So how is psychodynamic psychotherapy so effective? You will discover answers to that question throughout *Ensure*. But to begin, let's focus on the two aforementioned types of thinking.

The first is *logical thinking*, which we understand readil
is not effective in resolving emotional disorders. Logic does n
vince people to be happy, carefree, calm, kind, diligent...

The second is *non-logical*, which is foreign to most of us, but it is
the method used in therapy to reach our emotions. Sometimes it appears unclear, elusive, and, so to speak, dark. Therefore, we will now
attempt to illuminate it and the treatment.

The non-logical method of psychotherapy requires that patients
free associate, that is, they should say whatever comes to mind. At
first glance, that doesn't appear to be a logical way to solve problems.
However, to understand the power and effectiveness of free association, let's shift to circumstances other than psychotherapy, to see its
value from another perspective:

In 2002, two psychologists, Amos Tversky and Daniel Kahneman,
were awarded the Nobel Prize in Economic Sciences for discovering flaws that exist in people's *decision-making process*. What was
the method they used? They intentionally talked *freely, randomly*—in
effect, they *free associated—about various problems*, which they attempted to solve. But, they had a hidden agenda: to stir up hidden
flaws in their own thinking and those of people in general. They knew
that by talking loosely and freely they could disarm their defenses and
uncover the hidden flaws in their thinking.

They succeeded. Their discoveries have had revolutionary effects
in economics and other fields. *That's a great testimony to the power
of free association when used effectively.* The entire story and then
some is told in *Thinking, Fast and Slow*, Daniel Kahneman (Farrar,
Straus and Giroux, 2011).

Troublesome Emotions Can Be Reached Effectively Through Psychotherapy

You might be wondering, "Why so complicated?" Indeed there
are less complex treatments that help people straighten up and fly
right, meaning those methods treat symptoms or behaviors only,
without eliminating the causes of their problems. In those cases, the

problem, or its substitute, more than likely will return. That's known as *symptom substitution*, which occurs, for example, when people modify their eating habits without overcoming the underlying causes of their disorders—they might lose weight but then start to smoke. One person stopped smoking by eating excessively; after developing a weight problem, he shifted to eating sunflower seeds by the bagful; then, his tongue swelled up from becoming irritated—let's stop there.

In contrast, psychotherapy directs its efforts to the causes of disorders. In *Ensure,* the terms psychotherapy and therapy are used synonymously with psychodynamic or psychoanalytic psychotherapy; psychoanalysis was the original form of treatment from which all others were derived.

Ensure Explains What Patients Should Know and Do in Psychotherapy

Psychoanalysis and psychotherapy have helped people for over 100 years and have been the subject of thousands of books, almost all written for *psychotherapists'* use. ***Ensure is for patients' use.*** It draws from research studies, therapists' descriptions of what patients need to think about and do to succeed in treatment, and my own observations gathered from 44 years as a psychotherapist.

To maintain your trust in psychotherapy, please ignore those who undermine the treatment. Realize that Freud *scientifically* developed psychoanalysis, the "talking cure," through *natural observation* of his patients, a well-established scientific procedure that Albert Einstein, Charles Darwin, Stephen Hawking, and other geniuses used. Research—conducted by the likes of Jonathan Shedler, Lester Luborsky, Martin Seligman, and many other outstanding scientists—confirms psychoanalytic and psychodynamic principles established by Freud.

Much of the criticism of Freud revolves around some of the robust terms he used. That statement is not in his defense, but it is an effort /ou help yourself by rightfully believing in and using thera-
ntial power. Please keep in mind that Freud's 23 volumes,

in which he explained his psychoanalytic findings, earned him the Goethe Prize, a literary award, which also honors those authors who make outstanding creative and scientific contributions.

Derive the Full Benefits from Treatment

Now, an almost certain cure of your psychological disorder is attainable. Many studies show that of all psychotherapy patients, on the average, 70% accomplish their goals. If you're already in that category, use *Ensure* to help you zip along, make a smoother progression, and stave off regressions.

However, if you're in danger of falling into the dismal 30% category, learn more from *Ensure* about the critical importance of therapy's *introspection* process, which includes accessing, exploring, and effectively relating your thoughts, feelings, and memories to your therapist to help her assist you in overcoming your difficulties. By developing that skill, you can derive the full benefits of treatment.

Psychotherapists-in-training undergo psychotherapy treatment. However, *first they study therapy; then they become patients and learn about therapy through experience.* So, if therapists learn about therapy *before* undergoing treatment, then *patients should have at least some of that advantage too: Ensure's* aim is to provide a similar opportunity for patients.

Psychodynamic Psychotherapy's Effectiveness: It Employs a Powerful "Non-Logical" Method

You might be wondering, "Why aren't instructions provided to patients about free association and other aspects of therapy?" Well, ordinarily, providing precise instructions would be logical, but in psychotherapy, you and your therapist are developing an *emotional connection* to access the core of your problems, so those can be resolved. The logical and direct presentation of information, used in schools—the *didactic* method—would undermine the complex relationship between a patient and therapist, which is based on emotional factors, not intellectual ones.

Notwithstanding the above explanation, Freud did explain how patients should initiate treatment, which you will see in *Ensure's* Chapter Three. Until then, succinctly said, free association disarms the burdensome psychological defenses and pseudo-logical justifications we have erected over the years. We may say we drink alcohol to the point of passing out because our social circle demands such behavior, but free association may uncover our seeking an escape from another, larger problem. That technique unravels "blinders," which hide flaws and follies.

Let's take a look at one survey that revealed some of the benefits of therapy.

The 1995 *Consumer Reports* Survey— "Psychotherapy Usually Works"

The highlights of the 1995 *Consumer Reports* (CR) survey of its readers, regarding the outcomes of their psychotherapy, follow: 4,100 of CR's readers voluntarily responded to a 26-item questionnaire about their treatment from some combination of mental health professionals, family doctors, and support groups; 2,900 of those saw a mental health professional. The results, in summary, follow:

- Most people were very satisfied with the treatment they received.

- People who underwent psychotherapy without taking medication did as well as those who had medication plus psychotherapy. And, those who had more sessions improved more.

- The people who started treatment whose emotional condition was "very poor" when they began treatment (44%), said they now felt good. Those whose condition was "very poor" at the onset also improved significantly, but less than the "very poor" group.

- Almost all people felt at least some relief.[2]

In short, the study found that "psychotherapy usuall
that "most people do well in it."

A Further Reason to Trust
Psychodynamic Psychotherapy

Psychodynamic psychotherapy's special method, as we've seen, revolves around free association. Morton Reiser, a research psychiatrist at Yale found from his neuropsychiatric studies that, essentially, *memories are stored in our brains by being associated affectively one to another.* [3]

That is, several different memories become linked when one emotion is common to all. For example, a student's memories of his kindergarten teacher, mother, and aunt are each stored in separate regions of his brain. Since the *emotion of love was common to those three people*, the three memories will be *associated* in the neural network of the student's brain.

His findings strongly suggest that the effectiveness of psychotherapy's basic method, free association, is due to its *unraveling of associated memories*, or, in some cases and more importantly, *wrongly associated memories*—"mental log jams," so to speak—and ultimately enabling our healthy thoughts and feelings to emerge naturally.

Therapy Can Evict "Ghosts and Goblins,"
Leftovers from Childhood Still Haunting You

Free association quickly starts unraveling blinders that serve to conceal some ill conceived, immature, and naïve memories and thoughts. From childhood on, faulty methods of rearing lead to the blocking of our normal needs for love, affection, and then some. Wrongheaded "judges" misconstrue our aforementioned needs and taint those as being "reprehensible" and "unsavory." Consequently, we suppress our inner vigorous desires and force those into the back of our minds.

Imagine how often we restrain those normal, powerful drives—mainstays of life—having falsely learned they were objectionable. Some of society shudders, more often than not, at the mere mention of those unmentionables. However, those mental misconceptions become our minds' "ghosts and goblins." While out of sight, they are not out of our minds. They persevere in haunting and taunting us, and they wreak havoc on us.

To reduce that havoc, people pursue psychotherapy, because all other efforts have failed. Their ghosts and goblins carry on, before, during, and after Halloween. Paradoxically, all patients are reluctant to opening up and releasing those make-believe tormentors, fearing negative judgments will descend upon themselves for having harbored something so "loathsome." Therefore, too many people live with a Catch 22: By keeping their ghosts and goblins hidden, they maintain their illnesses; if they release them, they anticipate suffering from shame for having maintained them.

Psychotherapy offers a solution. With their therapists' aid, slowly and carefully, patients can reduce the influence of those inner pressures, and open up pathways of freedom from suffering.

But, here's where the Catch 22 comes in again: Every person in psychotherapy has an inner *resistance,* an automatic force that opposes the release of their ghosts and goblins. It's similar to driving a car with one foot on the accelerator and the other on the brake pedal. Psychotherapy treatment requires a continuous analysis of this contradictory force, which enables progress to take place.

Because resistances mobilize rapidly, patients should analyze those PDQ. Keep in mind: It's not therapy that necessarily works slowly. Free association works rapidly, so rapidly that resistance also builds up rapidly. A patient's resistance to being analyzed slows down the process. For example, if a medical patient has an infection, and he or she takes only one-fourth of the prescribed dose of an antibiotic, a cure certainly will be slow in coming, if it ever arrives at all.

There will be additional discussion of resistance further on in *Ensure.* But, for the time being, rather than yielding to resistance and thus stalemating the analysis, patients should analyze their resistance right from the get-go, to travel the psychotherapy road more efficiently, effectively, economically, and enjoyably. With that 4E formation in hand, let's turn to the next chapter, which explains how to move forward…

REFERENCES – TWO

1. Jonathan Shedler, (2010). "The Efficacy of Psychodynamic Psychotherapy," *American Psychologist*, Vol. 65, No. 2, 98-109.
2. "Mental Health: Does Therapy Help?" *Consumer Reports,* (November, 1995), pp. 734-736.
3. Morton F. Reiser, "Relationship of Psychoanalysis to Neuroscience," in *Textbook of Psychoanalysis,* ed. Edward Nersessian and Richard G. Kopff (Washington: American Psychiatric Press, 1996), pp. 605-633.

THREE

How to Begin Psychotherapy

Just Use Sigmund Freud's "Basic Rule"

FREUD MADE IT clear and easy to begin psychotherapy (psychoanalysis in his case) and continue on throughout it—just follow his *basic rule* of free association. For your own sake, adhere scrupulously to the following, his commentary about how to start treatment: "Please tell me what you know about yourself ... say whatever comes to mind."[1]

The master has spoken. Consider yourself launched. It is doable. However, despite your use of free association, roadblocks will surface, but *Ensure* explains how to negotiate those effectively. By using *Ensure's* information, you should be able to work more smoothly with your therapist, an experience that might open up or further your interest in developing the capacity to pursue additional strategies for therapy, as well as for life.

At this point, you might be wondering: "How do I talk about my relationships, which you previously encouraged me to do, and yet abide by the process of free association?" It's possible to start out talking about your relationships by free associating, and, if you drift to other issues, you can return at another point in time. There is also a matter of degree. Freud saw people up to six-days-per week. Nowadays, psychotherapy takes place one or more times weekly. So, as the teacher of tightrope walking said, "Do it by keeping your balance."

Regarding balance, the fewer the number of weekly sessions, the more verbally active a therapist is. The opposite is also true: more weekly sessions means the therapist is less active. The byword is teamwork—the two of you working it out together in a best-case scenario, explicitly for you. You'll both do it over and over again until you get it right.

Getting it right refers to being cooperative, again, which means developing and using the effective work ethic *Ensure* describes. A cooperative patient, seen on a once-per-week basis, will obtain better results than an unsophisticated one seen three- or four-times weekly.

Therapy's Road to a Cure Is Energized by Free Association

By becoming cooperative, patients can stay on psychotherapy's special road that leads to Shedler's definitive statement: "The goal of psychoanalytic psychotherapy is to loosen the bonds of past experience to create new life possibilities."[2] *First, free associate, then analyze resistance (over and over, again and again), and, **in time, when ready**, loosen the bonds of past experience.*

If you have difficulty loosening your bonds, try recalling how you did so in the past, when you actually let go of an old boyfriend, girlfriend, way of thinking, job, or any other involvements that you abandoned. You can free associate to remnants or memory traces of those people or situations, to retrieve your unique methods that helped shift your attitude back then. Use those methods to help let go of scenarios currently plaguing you. (See Chapter Four for further help in shifting your attitude.)

Perhaps you still have some hesitation about free associating, out of concern that you will be letting go of control of your mind. To be sure, it's quite the opposite—you'll actually let go of undesirable forces that unconsciously have been controlling and inhibiting your mind, your feelings, your desires, your creativity... Start adjusting to feeling better and thinking and feeling the way you choose, rather than maintaining your distress.

Free association is the best method we have to access and loosen burdensome bonds, which are somewhat the cause of what ails you—harsh memories, feelings, traumas, or relationships frozen into your mind and tormenting you. Free association unravels mental knots—burdensome thoughts seemingly tied into your mind—and helps access whatever has been doing you in, which sets the stage to loosen your bonds to those negative past experiences.

Although many people experience free associating as a golden opportunity, some feel threatened by it. If you fall into the latter category, shift your focus. See psychotherapy as your friend: welcome it, trust it, adjust to it… Realize everyone feels uncomfortable while trying to get well: medical treatments make unconventional incursions, such as sticking patients with needles or exploring their orifices. Psychotherapy can seem equally awkward. Yet, just saying whatever comes to mind is among the most harmless of medical procedures, and can be loads of fun, if you take the starch out of your psyche.

Psychotherapy's Special Road

The one special road you'll travel concerns identifying the "blinders" you've unwittingly developed and then disengaging them through free association. That entails accessing hidden flaws, namely: misuse of logic; errors in decision-making; drawing conclusions from minor premises; feelings of unworthiness, inadequacy, and whatever else ails you (more about those further on). Ultimately, the bonds will be loosened to those past experiences, which caused an emotional disorder, and you'll become free to choose any and all options for your life. To achieve a successful treatment, Shedler emphasizes fuller development of: relationships, talents and abilities, self-esteem, affect, sexual experiences, understanding self and others, and greater freedom and flexibility.[3]

Shedler recommends that we strive for more than symptom relief. Clearly, successful treatment opens up the doors to an enriched quality of life.

The Patient's Participation: Make a Wholehearted Effort

Be energetic: elaborate on your associations, feelings, thoughts, memories, fantasies... Be comprehensive, extensive, vigorous... Franz Kafka was a master at describing subtleties and nuances, leading him to gain profound insights. See some of his vivid expressions in his "Letter to Father": "You always reproached me... (and you joked) bitterly, that we were all too well off. That's why I could show my thanks to you for evereything only as a beggar does, and not by deeds."[4]

Kafka did not have the feeble and obliging attitude, "Okay, I'll tell you what comes to mind." He was grasping, groping, grappling in the corners and crevices of his memory to capture the essence of what he went through, how he felt he was treated, and how it all affected him.

Bring Forth Details

Ease your inner turmoil by recounting the details of your life's experiences and *fully express your feelings inherent in those memories:*

FIRST, THERE WILL BE UPHEAVAL, BUT THEN YOU'LL FEEL RELIEF!

Recalling all you can in the presence of your kind and caring therapist, especially while you are open and vulnerable, will create a *corrective emotional experience* for you: your harsh past experiences will be lessened, neutralized, by internalizing the healthy experience with your therapist. It's similar to the burning effect of acid being eased by diluting it with water.

People kid about how frequently therapists ask, "What are you feeling?"

While there is truth to it, and the humor is appreciated, in reality it's not a laughing matter: Therapists worth their salt know well that patients' benefits are directly related to the *depth and breadth of their recall of memories and feelings.* Again, consider Kafka's style: "I cannot remember your scolding me directly ... words of abuse flew all around me... You cursed without the slightest scruple, yet you condemned cursing in others and forbade it."[5]

As you free associate, Kafka-style, you and your therapist can spread before you the puzzling pieces of your *neurosis* (which generally refers to anxiety or depression; see Chapter Five). The taking apart of your puzzling problems, freeing yourself from them, and allowing your natural self to evolve, will necessitate your therapist's explaining many things en route. That process is termed the *mutative experience,* the series of statements made by your therapist, along with your cooperative efforts, which serve, in total, to bring about a cure. That process is more fully explained in Chapter Seven.

Relinquish Thought Control

Planning prior to a session, current events reporting, writing out dreams, reasoning, screening, and controlling or blocking out thoughts and feelings, while well-intentioned, actually prevent mental and emotional disturbances from being exposed and treated. If such control continues, deeply ingrained emotional problems stand little chance of being overcome. Freud cautioned patients to not prepare in advance what they were going to say, since such preparation was "only employed to guard against unwelcome thoughts cropping up."[6]

Be aware of controlling your thoughts. Instead of falling into that trap, rely on saying what comes to mind. Remember, resistance will persist throughout treatment, so repeatedly work on it. An ally of analyzing resistance is the working through process, also described by Freud: One must allow the patient time to become more conversant with this resistance... "This working-through of the resistances ... is a part of the work which effects the greatest changes in the patient."[7]

Talk to Your Therapist about These Important Issues:

Your Present Relationships

While Freud encourages patients to say whatever comes to mind, which is one key to your success in therapy, we return to another key, the discussion of relationships. You are encouraged to talk in detail to your therapist about your relationship issues. Draw from the information previously described in the Core Conflictual Relationship Theme (CCRT).

If you don't have any CCRT's to describe, then talk about why you don't have any. Recounting the details of the dialogue in your relationships might begin the process of becoming more effective in handling those. Dealing with difficult adult relationships by using methods left over from childhood just doesn't work. Don't resurrect naive methods that never worked to begin with. Those increase relationship difficulties.

Discuss details of your relationships with your therapist who might help you recognize your ineffective patterns. Never, ever give in to the impulse to feel overwhelmed and regress to primitive levels of coping. Contain your tensions, recount details to your therapist, and develop effective ways of relating. You may have found it a lot easier to regress than to progress. But, it's a lot harder staying regressed, and progressing is more rewarding.

Using ineffective methods when up against difficult situations and people makes things worse. Instead, take a timeout, count to ten, breathe deeply and hold it for four seconds, and most importantly, exhale... Then, take a walk or drink some water. Finally, tell your companion that you're very interested and concerned about what he or she said and felt, so you're going to think about it for a while and discuss it later on. When possible, talk it through with your therapist.

Your Relationship with Your Therapist and Your Past Relationships with Other People

To add depth and breadth to your therapy, consider Frieda Fromm-Reichmann's version of loosening your bonds with the past: "The most universal source of inner helplessness in adults... the need to repeat old patterns of relatedness and living... produces deep emotional insecurity in people."[8]

Fromm-Reichmann's above explanation of the "need to repeat old patterns of relatedness" directs us to understanding the connections between the *past* and *present*. A third dimension was introduced by

Karl Menninger, in *The Theory of Psychoanalytic Technique* (1958, Basic Books). He suggested that patients analyze *three levels of their relationships*: the *past*, with their parents; the *present*, with people currently in their lives; and, that with *their therapists*. Thus, you can form a "triangle" concerning relationships: the past, present, and therapy (that is, your relationship with your therapist). Repeatedly making comparisons in different contexts of the three corners of the triangle helps loosen bonds and fixations, which makes it possible for patients to develop.

Menninger's triangle adds depth, breadth, and insights, and it helps us understand what makes us psychologically what we are today and then enables us to function the way we want to. There's an old adage: "If we don't learn from the past, we are bound to repeat it in the future."

Be Actively Involved in the Treatment

Therapy is not an invasive procedure, as when surgeons perform operations or physicians inject medicine into us. Realize that you're attempting to re-educate your emotions. Instead of remaining passive, as in most medical procedures, actively apply what *Ensure* explains is necessary to do. Actively help your therapist make the treatment effective. Be in harmony with your therapist.

How to Be Active in Therapy

Both therapists and patients listen and talk. But patients must express associations and feelings, internalize insights, use those insights in their lives, and then return to sessions and discuss the ins and outs of having used what they took from the treatment. Repeatedly activating that sequence will help you restructure your mind and behavior. Being in accord with your therapist and active in the treatment also will help you become assertive.

Some Inside Tips

When your therapist says something to you, consider it and free associate to it—aloud, to the therapist—without agreeing or disagreeing. Use your therapist's input—make it into a catalyst for your development; loosen your defenses; open the closed doors of your mind. Do all of that, and you will emerge unburdened by excessive restrictions.

When your therapist says something, or asks a question, instead of responding with a "Yes" or a "No," free associate along the lines of openly questioning yourself to help explore your inner life: "How might this apply in some cases?" "How do I feel about it?" "Does this apply nowadays… when… where… how…?"

Therapists listen to what patients say, but they also listen for the mental mechanisms that patients use, for example, obsessing, or avoiding. Keep your mind open to how your therapist addresses your issues. Eventually you can learn to reflect back on yourself in a manner incorporating your therapist's techniques.

By reflecting, you become mentally active in treatment. That is a critical step in the emotional learning process. Karen Horney said, "It is scarcely an overstatement that, apart from the analyst's competence, it is the patient's constructive activity that determines the length and outcome of an analysis."[14]

Please… if you are a tattoo person, tattoo Horney's statement into the forefront of your mind. Always remember that she advocated "the patient's constructive activity." Horney's *constructive activity* means that you should *open up*; *bring forth* associations; *recall* dreams; *free associate* to the elements in your dreams; *use new and effective ways of being* that your therapist might recommend; and, *pursue* healthy ways. Never ignore, but instead, always free associate to every gift: namely, slips of the tongue and other errors you make. According to Freud, the latter are *portholes into the unconscious*, so those are a special opportunity to free associate and gain the most dynamic understanding of the depths of your psyche. Being active in therapy will help restructure your mind, create inner freedom, and enable you to become effective in relationships.

REFERENCES – THREE

1. Sigmund Freud, J. Strachey, ed. and trans., *The Stanua.* of the Complete Psychological Works of Sigmund Freud (London: Hogarth Press, 1957), Vol. 1, (originally published in 1916), pp. 134-135.
2. Jonathan Shedler, *That Was Then, This is Now: Psychoanalytic sychotherapy for the Rest of Us,* 2006; 21. http://jonathan@shedler. com.
3. Jonathan Shedler, (2010). "The Efficacy of Psychodynamic Psychotherapy," *American Psychologist,* Vol. 65, No. 2, 98-109.
4. Franz Kafka, *Letter to Father.* (Czech Republic: Vitalis, 2005), pp. 31-33.
5. Ibid., p. 25.
6. Sigmund Freud, J. Strachey, ed. and trans., "On Beginning the Treatment," *The Standard Edition of the Complete Psychological Works of Sigmund Freud* (London: Hogarth Press, 1957), Vol. XII (originally published in 1916), p. 136.
7. Ibid., pp. 155-156.
8. Frieda Fromm-Reichmann, *Psychoanalysis and Psychotherapy.* (Chicago: University of Chicago Press, 1959).

FOUR

Some Guidelines
Work Towards Mental Health

What Comprises A Cure?

2,000 YEARS AGO: Carved into the façade of the temple of Apollo, atop the upper slopes of Mount Parnassus in Delphi, are the words, "Know Thyself," which expressed the ancient Greeks' wisdom, their ultimate counsel for health.

Over 100 Years Ago: Freud felt that the ultimate sign of a cure was a person's ability to *lieb und arbeit*—love and work. Along those lines, as quoted on page *i* in *Ensure,* Freud felt the aim of treatment is "...to secure the best possible psychological conditions for the function of the ego."

In the 1940s: Carl Rogers stated that the goal of treatment and mental health was to be free from *internal blockage.*

In the 1950s: Heinz Hartmann said that therapy's goal was the development of a *conflict-free sphere of ego functioning.*

In the 1990s: Lester Luborsky banked heavily on *mastery of internal conflicts and relations.*

In 2012: Most recently, Shedler and colleagues presented a poignant summary of the *healthy personality.* To illustrate the scope of his coverage, some highlights follow, regarding areas concerned: "relationships, intimacy, morality, comfortably sociable, effective assertion, likable, satisfying sex lives, understanding, emotional maturity,

rm goals and ambition..."[1]

According to Shedler, we all have our work cut out for us. He wants us to have a healthy inner life and to be effective in the world. Keep his and the others' guidelines in mind as you proceed through therapy.

Know Where You're Going: Areas to Assess Progress

The Koran explains, if you don't know where you are going, any road will take you there. Be aware that psychological growth in therapy is a work in progress. Discuss your progress, that is, from time to time, but don't overdo it. Luborksy and Grenyer[2] developed measures for assessing the ways patients change during the course of psychotherapy, the essence of which follows:

Impulse Control: First We Analyze, Then We React

It is necessary to contain your impulses and avoid *acting-out*. The latter refers to taking action on impulses regarding significant issues or desires and emotions, without first discussing those with your therapist.

Although giving in to the impulse *to be overwhelmed* may not be your problem, it does occur frequently in people with emotional disorders. The following exclamations might help you recognize that problem: "I can't take it anymore." "There's just no way to deal with her." "My boss is unbearable." Those are cries of helplessness, which block the development of new and constructive ways to stay the course.

Again, for emphasis, acting-out on impulses, without talking the issues through with a therapist, is damaging, and it slows therapeutic progress.

If acting-out persists, it can destroy treatment, as sure as Freud developed psychoanalysis. Hold impulses in check and talk them through. It's clear: acting-out is the opposite of analyzing, so it goes totally against a basic principal in psychotherapy: "First we analyze, then we react."

Latent Learning

Psychotherapy is an educational process, which revolves around our emotions. Therefore, therapists create an atmosphere in which patients can evelop themselves; therapists don't do something to someone, the way dentists drill teeth. As such, progress is not always immediately recognized. There are ups and downs as new ways are being developed and tried on for size. Generally, don't dwell on temporary highs and lows, since that might inhibit you.

It's fairly well known that William James asserted, "We learn to swim in the winter and ice skate in the summer." Meaning, of course, upon first learning something, it's not immediately apparent that we actually learned it. But, despite no evidence of learning having taken place, according to James, some has, which he viewed as latent or dormant. The proof will surface in time.

Again, here and there, analyze where you have been and where you're hoping to go. It's best to raise that issue with your therapist and explore it through free association, to access your inner feelings and thoughts that are relevant.

Freedom from Feelings of Suffering

Mental or emotional suffering is not easy to overcome as we have previously discussed. Oddly enough, the need to suffer is ingrained in many people, and they begin to accept it as if it were part of them. In those cases, their mental suffering is known as *masochism*, a condition in which people derive obvious or hidden gratification from their distress. Later on in *Ensure,* you will discover more about how some people accept and gain hidden gratification from such suffering, and how that condition can be overcome.

Steadily overcoming the acceptance of suffering is an important undertaking in therapy. Prehistoric people did whatever they desired. Civilized people abide by the laws of society, requiring that we regulate but never obliterate desires. We suffer even when we suppress them. We have to develop the ability to express and direct our emotions effectively.

In *Civilization and Its Discontents,* Freud explained how that process of restraining desires started with the onset of civilization, which revolves around laws and our curtailing of desires. Carried to an extreme, reining in our desires can cause us to develop internal conflicts and stress, resulting in the outbreak of neuroses. However, unraveling and undoing excessively burdensome psychological restraints opens up the opportunity for people to become effective in fulfilling their desires, and thus freeing themselves from neuroses.

Mastery of Interpersonal Relations
Emotional disorders are mainly the result of chronic relationship problems. Therefore, progress in this area is critical, as explained throughout *Ensure.*

Self-Understanding
Understanding oneself from a psychodynamic psychotherapy perspective is essential for progress. That form of therapy will help you understand the interconnections of your past behavior, your current life, your relationship with your therapist, your causes of inner conflicts, and your symptoms.

Along those lines, Anna Freud described how "patients in therapy routinely are self-observant, [but] antagonistic to analysis, and are observers of their own egos..."[3] In short, she meant that patients must reflect back on themselves, but at the same time analyze their opposition to doing so. That opposition is a force that automatically resists therapy, because unconsciously patients feel the treatment is somewhat of an intruder.

Consequently, according to Anna Freud, patients must analyze their own egos [their selves], "in that the defensive operations in which it is perpetually engaged are carried on unconsciously and can be brought into consciousness only at considerable expenditure of effort ..."[4] Of course, her phrase, "considerable expenditure of effort," refers to the ongoing analysis of resistance.

All the foregoing, and the entire text of *Ensure* as well, should not be considered an academic task in which its information is to be memorized. Use *Ensure* to help you adjust to therapy; to develop an open and cooperative frame of mind; and, to enjoy the process, which is probably highly different from any other you have ever experienced. Eventually, you and your therapist will find a rhythm suitable for the two of you, which can be highly rewarding.

Self-Control and the Capacity for Constructive Actions

Here's where the big payoff takes place: Containing your tensions and impulses enables the analytic process to take place and opens up new pathways of thinking, feeling, and behaving. Progress in this area puts you on the royal road to a cure. There will be more covered for this stage in Chapter Five.

Shift Your Attitude and Make Progress

For progress in psychotherapy, we turn again to another frequently quoted saying by James, "The greatest discovery of any generation is that a human can alter his life by altering his attitude." We touched on this issue previously, but now we can elaborate.

If you feel uncertain about how to change your attitude to help let go of an idea, relationship, or feeling, just reflect on the countless times you've done so already, throughout your life. Consider how you shifted your attitude and made changes in the following ways: letting go of one friendship and developing a new one; changing your preferences for clothing, books, movies, sports; shifting religious beliefs; making a career choice; or changing jobs.

Start contemplating those issues, by asking yourself diverse but relevant questions. Then, free associate to discover and use constructive ways that were involved in having shifted your attitude in the past. It might help you to let go of non-productive ways as well.

Pose questions in therapy to yourself such as, "What were the circumstances and the details of my prior situations that enabled me to 'let go'?" "What were the significant factors?" "What feelings did I have?"

"What were the outcomes in each scenario?" Explore those questions, again, through free association. By unearthing details, you'll make discoveries about what did and didn't work; apply those findings to current situations you're encountering.

Realize, you're not a stranger to shifting your attitude; we all do it repeatedly. It's a matter of gaining *insight*—obtaining a new understanding, primarily about yourself and people—into what enabled you to shift your attitude in the past. Free association can help you to access that powerful force, the shifting of attitude, which leads to progress.

The Main Curative Factors in Psychodynamic Therapy

So, how can people achieve a cure? What and where is the roadmap to such happiness? Luborsky and his colleagues reviewed transcripts of sessions of the more improved patients versus the less improved, from which they developed eight main curative factors.[5] Six are patient factors and two are therapist factors, all of which you will find below. The number next to each factor pertains to the degree of its importance.

So, "Factor 1" is the most important and "Factor 8" the least. Please pay special attention to Factor 1 below. It's a mainstay of treatment.

Patient: Main Curative Factor

Factor 1. *"Patient's experience of a helping relationship."* There are two questions regarding this factor: "Is the therapist effectively implementing a helping relationship?" (For this latter question, see below, under "Therapist… Factor 2.") And, "Is the patient able to experience it as helping?"

Some patients are open to being helped. For example, *after leaving a session, they take what the therapist said and apply it in their lives. Upon returning for their next session, they explore the results with their therapists.* Clearly, patients who are open to their therapist's help absorb information from them and work with it.

33

For another example: I faced a disturbing situation during the course of my own therapy. In response to my plight, my analyst said. "Do whatever needs to be done." I took that brief but powerful statement, applied it, and it saved the day for me. I have repeatedly used and benefitted from that attitude ever since, so I'm still getting my money's worth.

Yet, oddly enough, some patients, despite pursuing therapy, are not willing or even able to participate in such teamwork. Their up-bringing lacked the experience of absorbing help from someone and working with what they learned. In therapy, it's as if each session starts anew for those "loners." What you and your therapist have established in past sessions, should be carried forward and built upon in new sessions; keep the momentum going.

For therapists, it seems that what they have told such patients never took place. Along those lines, an extremely important source of feedback for a patient is what the therapist's experience has been in working with said patient. The therapist might experience the patient as being constructive or destructive, passive or assertive, involved or indifferent, self-absorbed or interested in others. Pay heed to these gems and work with them.

Closed-off people need to develop openness to a helping person. Instead of yielding to the impulse to be detached, they need to contain it and participate actively with what their therapists have put forth, right in their sessions. They need to make a conscious effort to take hold of what they're told. They can start by repeating aloud what was said to them. Then, they can discuss it. They can say anything to get a new pathway going.

It's simple enough: if you're even slightly in the detached category, don't ignore what your therapist says, but give it attention, entertain it, consider it. Grapple with the issue. You might say, "I never thought about that before... let me see... I did act in that fashion last week"—and then, yes! Free associate. In childhood, if you were not helped to enjoy teamwork, therapy is the place to develop that important capacity.

Get involved! If you're closed off, triple your efforts to redirect yourself. If you're inner-directed, become outer-directed; convert yourself from an innie to an outie. Retain what your therapist says; put it to use after the session is over; discuss how you used the input; open up new abilities of relating and working with a helping person.

Along those aforementioned lines, neurology gave us a new gift, *neuroplasticity*. In short, new findings show that certain areas in our brains become larger as we repeat specific behaviors governed by those brain areas. The larger that area in the brain becomes, the more capability it develops… the more capability, the more we can do… on to becoming a veritable genius in that domain.

And that's not my talking in a brainless way—research backs it up. That's made clear in the entire issue of *Time*, October 22, 2013, "Secrets of Genius: Discovering the Nature of Brilliance."

Unquestionably, the sooner patients put into action those things developed in treatment, the sooner they will reap rewards. Any new behavior, such as "being open," implemented over and over, again and again, throughout the course of therapy and life after treatment, will build new pathways in the brain that become a launching pad for new and healthy ways of being.

Don't wait until the last day of treatment to get it right. It's not going to happen that way. Along those lines, psychotherapy usually has three stages: a *beginning*, wherein patients acclimate; a *middle*, where they get down to the meat and potatoes; and, *termination*, in which patients work through issues stirred up by the finalization process. This is a general statement, which doesn't consider time limits, because each person is different. However, by realizing there are three stages, it should help you adjust to the process.

A neat example of the power inherent in working at things and finding a way comes to us from Betty Edwards. In *Drawing on the Right Side of the Brain,* she describes how the lef
controls language and dominates the right side, w
ativity. Edwards helps her students overcome th
drawing by having them turn the drawing they are
side down. Then, the left sides of their brains cann

36

"upside-down language." By being disarmed, it can no longer bully the right side. Consequently, her students' drawings improved notably. And, as a bonus, the capacities of the right sides of their brains developed—remarkable stuff.

Factor 2 appears in the section below: "Therapist: Main Curative Factors."

Factor 3. ***"Patient's gains in self-understanding."*** This is the patient's part in the joint search for acquiring understanding. It is the active process of reflection, or looking into oneself. That process is a form of the Socratic method, developed 2,000 years ago by Socrates. He posed questions to his fellow citizens in an effort to stimulate them to *reflect* upon their "false beliefs" and help them to start the process of unraveling their unfounded ideas and initiating their enlightenment.

That process of reflection is an essential part of what is termed the *heuristic method,* the mainstay of psychotherapy. That method involves patients reflecting back on themselves, through free association, to make self-discoveries. The heuristic method, in a sense, is the opposite of the didactic method, described earlier. The latter directly instructs, or teaches, students what they are to learn. Didactics usually work best when the contents are of a logical and essentially concrete nature, as in math, geography, and so forth, which the intellect manages well. The heuristic method works best when attempting to re-educate the emotions, which requires the special process employed by psychotherapy.

Free association comes naturally for some people. Others, those who run a tight ship, are specialists in talking only about the here and now, specific problems, or current events. Dwelling on a topic does not open the important nuances of people's minds and lives.

To some degree, being reluctant to using free association, apart from being resistance, is due to our using *convergent thinking,* or "just stating the facts." Exclusive use of the latter form of thinking is a result of seeking the one and only right answer.

Divergent thinking, in contrast, is the basis of creativity and characteristically lets our thoughts diverge: "How many different ways are there to see or do this or that?" "What are the many possibilities?"

Convergers need to become divergers, at least for openers in therapy. Become a diverger and make progress in therapy by helping the right side of your brain and your brain's creative capacity develop.

Factor 4. *"Patient's decrease in pervasiveness of relationship conflicts."* Relationship conflicts cause most neuroses. As discussed previously, the biggest sources of stress from life's changes, leading to psychiatric and physical illnesses, concern relationships. In order of severity, they are: death of a spouse, divorce, and separation. As patients make progress in therapy, their inner conflicts lessen and their effectiveness in relationships improves. (This issue, "Factor 4," is discussed throughout *Ensure*.)

Factor 5. *"Patient's capacity to internalize treatment benefits."* This is the person's ability to make, internalize, and hold onto treatment gains. For example, many people lose significant amounts of weight, only to regain the pounds shortly afterward. When they tell their friends, "I lost 30 pounds," some reply, "Don't worry, you'll find them."

However, by first reducing inner conflicts through therapy, patients become free from inner tensions, making it possible for them to internalize treatment benefits. Then, they not only can make progress, but they are able to hold onto their gains.

Factor 6. *"Patient's learning of greater tolerance for his or her thoughts and feelings."* Intolerance of thoughts and feelings is where mental problems can begin. For example—an extreme and hypothetical one to make the point—a father might punish his son by taking his favorite toy away from him. The boy, as furious as can be, silently wishes that his father "drop dead." If at some point close in time to the boy's silent wish, the father involuntarily complies, that would be the end of the father but just the beginning of the boy's grief.

The boy's "magical thinking" erroneously might have led him to believe that his secret wish caused his father to die. Having no tolerance for that frightening thought, his mind would have repressed it into his unconscious, so he no longer had to consciously struggle with it. Unfortunately, he would have some powerful and unshakable feelings of guilt, probably for the rest of his life. Hopefully, he would consider pursuing psychodynamic therapy to develop a tolerance for his thoughts and feelings, and unearth and let go of his immature distortions.

Factor 7. *"Patient's motivation to change."* People have to be motivated to gain a cure in psychotherapy, so motivation would be a main factor. But, it is surprising not to see it higher on the list in importance, perhaps explained by some people's motivation improving due to the successful operation of the seven other factors, especially Factors 1, 2, 3, and 4.

Therapist: Main Curative Factors

Factor 2. *"Therapist's ability to understand and respond."* This is the therapist's ability to understand and manage the relationship with the patient. There is much to be considered, along the aforementioned lines, which goes beyond the scope of *Ensure*. However, if patients have some doubts, they can discuss those with their therapists and, if necessary, pursue a second opinion.

Factor 8. *"Therapist's ability to offer a technique that is clear, reasonable, and likely to be effective."* This is "the clarity, reasonableness, and expected effectiveness of the therapist's technique." [6]

The above summary shows that six of the eight main curative factors in psychotherapy are in the patients' hands. That finding is not surprising, considering therapy is a process involving the re-education of the emotions. Someone once said, "There's no such thing as teaching, there's only learning." In short, we cannot inject thoughts into someone's mind; learners must actively participate in learning. The good news is what patients take from the treatment is in direct relation to what effort they put in. That is why I wrote *Ensure*: *Psychotherapy results are primarily in patients' hands, so they will be much better off if they understand and are prepared for what psychotherapy entails.*

Distinctive Features in Psychodynamic Psychotherapy

In 2000, two researchers, Matthew Blagys and Mark Hilsenroth, reviewed the literature on the process and techniques of psychodynamic psychotherapy, which pinpointed seven features in that treatment that distinguished it from other types of therapy. [7]

Focus on Affect and Expression of Emotion

Explore the full range of your emotions: Handled effectively, they're exhilarating; mishandled, they're grievous. Getting in touch with all feelings, including bodily sensations, is essential. Fully describe your emotional and physical feelings, including muscle tightness, gastric distress... Talking about them leads to well-being.

Exploration of Attempts to Avoid Distressing Thoughts and Feelings

The following behaviors are damaging to treatment: missing sessions, arriving late, or being evasive (for further details see the quote from Freud at the beginning of Chapter Three in *Ensure*). If your therapist pinpoints those or other behaviors that undermine treatment, be open to discussing them. Your therapist is your ally; those behaviors are your undoing.

Also, let go of unnecessary sensitivities; don't get your back up if your therapist addresses issues that bog you down. Thin-skinned people force therapists to be roundabout when making a point, which, obviously, extends the quality and length of treatment. Patients need to remember that their therapists are there to help them, and some of their statements are about patients' *self-defeating behaviors*, the *mishandling of themselves*. Therapists' comments are not criticisms or attacks on the patients' egos, their selves. After all, therapists are there, in part, to help people grow their egos.

Identification of Recurring Themes and Patterns

This feature concerns the process of identifying and exploring recurring themes and patterns regarding your self-concept, thoughts, feelings, relationships, and experiences. Regarding thoughts, the range is nearly infinite, if you open up to the possibilities: ideas, notions, perceptions, speculations, topics, beliefs.... Give those a chance and they will just "pop into your mind." Spontaneity is the key.

Freud referred to the "red thread," the underlying theme that runs through all of a person's free associations. For example, a person might bring forth thoughts, fantasies, dreams, and the like, over time, and *dependency* might appear as the subject in each: In short, be on the lookout for your own red threads and analyze them.

Discussion of Past Experience

Early experiences affect our current lives and should be explored, since determining how our past affects the present is critical to gaining a cure. Some troublesome thoughts, occurrences, or wishes are *repressed,* that is, blocked out of our awareness. Although forgotten, they seethe and can boil over, meaning they erupt into a psychological disorder. In short, patients need to overcome their forgetting, their amnesia for childhood.

This might seem to pose a difficulty, but it doesn't have to be one. Yes, to gain a cure theoretically requires overcoming childhood amnesia, but that is not fully possible. Therefore, hypothetically, cures would not be attainable. However, patients resurrect forgotten memories, particularly those concerning their parents, when those are re-enacted in the relationship with therapists. Analysis of the latter, a process known as the *analysis of the transference,* can be extraordinarily powerful.

An example of the above follows: If a man talks to his therapist about his dependency problem, he opens it up for analysis. But asking his therapist to tell him how to get a job, how to interview, how to write a resume... *re-enacts* his dependency problem, in the transference, as it was originally set in childhood. The past has come alive in the present and can be seen, heard, experienced, and, as such, has become more capable of being analyzed and overcome.

Analysis of the transference is extremely valuable because that analysis enables patients to see, feel, and re-experience the past. Recollections from memories are valuable, but they lack the richness of analyzing real feelings developed in the transference, which is so necessary for a cure. Those past experiences, revived and relived with the therapist in the transference, enable patients to rid themselves of distortions and other harsh effects from childhood, regarding their parents or other people.

Many experts believe the most essential aspect of therapy revolves around patients discussing their relationships with their therapists. Freud himself set forth the principle that analysis of the transference can lead to a cure. (See Chapter Seven for further discussions of this issue.)

Focus on Interpersonal Relations

This feature involves patients discussing with their therapists the nature of their relationships with people, which we touched upon previously, to discover how those affect the patient and others. Theodore Reik's *On Love and Lust* and Erik Berne's *Transactional Analysis* explain how relationships go awry through misalignments between two people, for example, when one relates like an adult and the other like a child.

It follows: There is no substitute in therapy for talking about relationships. If you have none at all, explore why you currently don't have any. Talk about your past relationships; if you didn't have any in the past, then certainly you can talk about what you imagine in your fantasies. Fully develop your capacity to do *whatever must be done in and out of therapy* to bring about the maximum enjoyment in your relationships.

Exploration of Fantasy Life

Patients should recount their daydreams, concerns, wishes, goals, fleeting thoughts, and impulses. Consequently, verbalizing and working with those imaginings and their influence on you will be important in helping you stay on therapy's road.

You might be wondering, "Why the importance of exploring unrealistic fantasies?" For several reasons that will become apparent, for you as an individual, in your own treatment. But for now, the main reason is that fantasies are rooted in the deepest levels of everyone's psyche. The exploration of fantasies will enrich your therapy by directing you to the core of your issues.

Focus on Your Relationship with Your Therapist

This refers to the identification and analysis of recurring themes in that relationship, which, again, is the transference. That refers to patients' projecting aspects of their relationships with their parents onto their therapists. Psychodynamic psychotherapy holds analysis of the transference as a crucial, irreplaceable part of the treatment.

The burden of the analysis of transference falls on the therapist. But, to fully benefit, patients need to allow themselves to feel what their therapists say about them. In Anna Freud's opinion, "perhaps the most powerful instrument in the analyst's hand: the interpretation of the transference. By transference we mean all those impulses [from the relationship between the child and the parent(s)] and are now merely revived...."[8]

Therefore, it is of primary importance that patients access hidden feelings from childhood toward their mothers and fathers. That process is another major factor in gaining a cure.

Undo the Taboo on Feelings

The following admonishments comprise much of society's credo for youngsters: "Zip your lip"; "Hold your tongue"; "Keep your feelings to yourself"; "Don't open your mouth to me"; "His blood is boiling"; "Master your feelings"; "Stew in your juice"; "Sit on thorns"; "Keep your skeletons in the closet"; "Hold your breath"; "Turn blue in the face"; "Wait your turn"; "Draw a long breath"; "I'll give you something to cry about"; "Don't be sad"; "Don't be lonely"; "Don't be fresh"; "Absence makes the heart grow fonder"; "Don't feel hurt"...

The above harsh assertions have passed through far too many children's ears and minds. Essentially they dictate, *"Don't feel."* Do you think Freud was on to something concerning repression being the cause of emotional suffering?

Of course, at times those sayings have importance. Nevertheless, people with neuroses suffer from the effects of excessive repression. The extreme, the demolishing of children's feelings and individuality, is vividly portrayed in the 1982 film, *Pink Floyd: The Wall,* written by Roger Waters. Roger Ebert had this to say about it:

> Students on a conveyor belt are fed into the blades [of a meat grinder] that extrude them as ground meat. In the process, the students lose their faces behind blank masks ... Message: Education produces mindless creatures suitable as cannon fodder or the puppets of fascists.[9]

Being able to recover buried feelings is one of many rewards derived from psychotherapy. That prize opens up freedom of choices. Emanuel Hammer's depiction of the "Therapeutic Goal" follows: "Insight must be taken beyond understanding to a fuller emotional acceptance of the impulses. This self acceptance... replaces self condemnation and... gives way to self tolerance."[10]

Hammer also puts it succinctly: "Therapy should move toward the earthy—the meat and potatoes of real feelings."[11] He counsels us to turn to musicians, artists, poets, and other creative people to learn how they reach emotions at the deepest levels, a talent we can all strive to develop. Some examples follow:

Upon hearing the resounding words, "Mine eyes have seen the glory of the coming of the Lord ...," from *The Battle Hymn of the Republic,* we feel transported. When Marlon Brando roars, "Stelluuuhhh," in the movie *The Streetcar Named Desire,* it's as if he were a lion. Thomas Wolfe's yearnings from *You Can't Go Home Again* are contagious: "Could I make tongue say more than tongue could utter ... could I weave into immortal denseness some small brede of words ... some hundred thousand magic words that were as great as all my hunger, and hurl the sum of all my living out upon three hundred pages..."[12]

43

And in *Of Time and the River* Thomas Wolfe's lamenting about his mangled, unfulfilled desires re-awakens our longings: "Immortal love, alone and aching in the wilderness, we cried to you: You were not absent from our loneliness."[13]

While touching upon human emotional depth, suffering, and loneliness, we dare not omit these lines from Samuel Taylor Coleridge's "Rime of the Ancient Mariner":

> Alone, alone, all, all alone,
> Alone on a wide, wide sea!
> And never a saint took pity on
> My soul in agony.[14]

Deep within us lies a "seething cauldron of desire," according to Freud. Fear of that desire leads to a suppression of it, which takes its toll. Unravel resistances and defenses formed in childhood, unleash your yearnings and creative energy, and open pathways towards fulfillment of your desires. In every therapy session access those feelings within you, and express them vigorously as artists do. There is no substitute for feeling.

REFERENCES - FOUR

1. Westen, D., Shedler, J., Bradley, B., & DeFife, J.A., (2012). "An Empirically Derived Taxonomy for Personality Diagnosis: Bridging Science and Practice in Conceptualizing Personality." *Am J Psychiatry*, 169:3, 282.
2. B.F.S. Grenyer & L. Luborsky, "Dynamic Change in Psychotherapy: Mastery of Interpersonal Conflicts," *Journal of Consulting and Clinical Psychology, (1966), pp. 411-416.*
3. Anna Freud, *The Ego and the Mechanisms of Defense.* (New York: International Universities Press, 1946), pp. 31-32.
4. Ibid., p. 32.
5. Lester Luborsky, Paul Crits-Christoph, Jim Mintz, & Arthur Auerbach, *Who Will Benefit from Psychotherapy?: Predicting Therapeutic Outcomes* (New York: Basic Books, 1988), pp. 163-164.
6. Luborsky, et al., p. 165.
7. Blagys, M.D. & Hilsenroth, M.J. (2000). "Distinctive Activities of Short-Term Psychodynamic-Interpersonal psychotherapy: A Review of the Comparative Psychotherapy Process Literature." *Clinical Psychology: Science and Practice, 7*, pp. 167-188.
8. Anna Freud, *The Ego and the Mechanisms of Defense.* (New York: International Universities Press, 1946), pp. 31-32.
9. Roger Waters, *Pink Floyd: The Wall* (London: Pink Floyd Music Publishers, 1982), http://www. rogerebert.com/reviews/great-movie-pink-floyd-the-wall- 1982, p. 2.
10. Emanuel Hammer, *Reaching the Affect: Style in the Psychodynamic Therapies* (New Jersey: Jason Aronson, 1990), p. 25.
11. Ibid., p. 20.
12. Thomas Wolfe, *You Can't Go Home Again* (New York: Simon and Schuster, 1940), preface.
13. Thomas Wolfe, *Of Time and the River* (New York: Scribner Classics, 1935/1963), preface.
14. Samuel Taylor Coleridge, "The Rime of the Ancient Mariner," *Library of World Poetry,* (New York: Chatham River Press, 1798/1987), p. 647.

FIVE

Overcoming Obstacles

Resistance: The Major Roadblock

TO BRIEFLY RECAP: We've addressed psychotherapy's special method, free association, which takes patients down a special road. Patients are eager to take that trip as rapidly as possible. After all, they seek help in overcoming unresolved emotional problems.

However, it appears to be an absurdity that patients who avidly pursue therapy simultaneously resist it. Previously, an analogy was presented that portrayed the contradiction: stepping on the accelerator of an auto with one foot, while pressing the other foot on the brake pedal. However, allow Freud to describe this paradox: "The patient who is suffering so much from his symptoms puts up a struggle against the person who is helping him. The patient's resistance is of many sorts, extremely subtle and hard to detect..."[1]

Once you discover the nature of your resistances and defenses, "blinders," you can start removing that blockage by analyzing it. However, *all people* unwittingly cling somewhat to their emotional disorders, necessitating an ongoing analysis of resistances and defenses over the entire special road to a cure.

Soften and Loosen Resistance to Release Your Natural Self

Perhaps the following concrete example will help clarify the importance of a long-lasting analysis of resistance: A man stepped on something while walking on the beach, which caused a laceratio and subsequent infection in his toe. The infection persisted despite cleansing the wound and employing antibiotics, x-rays, and exploratory surgery.

Subsequently, the man consulted a seasoned general practitioner, whose advice was, "Soak it! Soak it! Soak it!" The patient complied, and after two days, a wooden sliver popped out of the lesion and all was well again (wood does not show on x-ray). Obviously, the soaking softened the tissue surrounding the deeply embedded splinter, loosened it, and then it dislodged.

Similarly, analyzing resistance over the course of therapy softens, loosens, and dislodges embedded negative past experiences, which enables people to move on in life in the manner described above by Shedler.[2] There will be more to follow about resistance.

Develop Psychotherapy's Special Methods ASAP

Is there a person who has not heard the saying? "It's mind over matter." That's true to some extent. Often, if you "Make up your mind, you can do it." However, nowadays we have to add, "Do it, and that will develop not only your mind but your brain as well." Previously, we touched upon *neuroplasticity*, the term for the process in which new behaviors create new nerve pathways in the brain and, strikingly, their functional capacities become increased.

In *The Brain That Changes Itself,*[3] Norman Doidge extensively documents the phenomenon of neuroplasticity with astonishing case histories. In many of those cases, innovative treatments overcame stroke and other formerly incurable brain disorders.

Eleanor Maguire demonstrated a clesar and vivid example of the brain's neuroplasticity in a study of taxi drivers in London:

Taxi drivers given brain scans by scientists at University College London had a larger hippocampus compared with other people.... The scientists also found part of the hippocampus grew

47

taxi drivers spent more time on the job. There
a definite relationship between the navigating
taxi driver and the brain changes.[4]

In short, the above research findings point to the importance of, again, using psychotherapy's special methods as soon as possible. As you do so prudently, new connections will develop for new areas of thinking, feeling, and behaving. Consequently, the sizes of the related areas in your brain will start increasing.

Taking new actions, mental or physical, will expand your brain's capacity to handle even more learning. The ramifications are enormous. Please remember, *the more you do, the more you will be able to handle, and the more you are able to handle, the more you can do.*

The mere process of being active will develop brain areas that control those behaviors inherent in those activities, enabling you to become more effective in life! Nature has guaranteed that for us, according to the most current scientific findings.

Overcome Inhibitions to Initiating New Behaviors by Analyzing Your Resistance to Change

Psychodynamic psychotherapy requires one or more weekly sessions, necessitating substantial financial, emotional, and time commitments over an extended period. As touched upon previously, despite such huge efforts on the part of patients, the treatment revolves around an analysis of their resistances to treatment—resistance on the part of *all* patients. It's a fundamental part of the treatment. Therefore, the phenomenon of resistance and its analysis are now more fully explained:

In the index to Freud's 23 volumes, there are 51 listings for resistance, as in its reference to "repetition," "transference," "disguised as eagerness," "frustration," and more. The topic of resistance occurs throughout Freud's writings, and it surfaces in the nooks and crannies of everyone's treatment. That's the bad news. *The good news is that analysis of resistance can help overcome your resistance to change, and it leads to a cure.*

Freud's Commentary about the Types of Resistance

Let's proceed directly to the original source, Freud, concerning the types of resistance: "All the forces that oppose the work of recovery.... The gain from illness [described below as a *secondary gain*]... The 'unconscious sense of guilt'"... Fear if the ego approaches the repressed material."[5] So, as you tackle resistance, you directly begin to unravel the above-mentioned areas of your difficulty.

For an example of secondary gain, Freud recounted a story about a lieutenant hospitalized because he was suffering from a traumatic war neurosis. The officer recited a poem on a particular occasion, originally written as follows:

> But where is it decreed, I ask, that out of all I should alone be left, my fellow for me fall? Whoever of you falls, for me that man doth die; And I—am I alone to live? Why should I?[6]

But upon reading the poem, the lieutenant made a slip of the tongue in the closing line, and said, instead, "Why should not I?" The slip revealed his hidden wish to live, and not to die, the opposite point as written in the poem.

Slips of the tongue reveal hidden wishes, thoughts, or motives. It follows that the soldier's traumatic neurosis provided a secondary gain, since it kept him in the hospital, alive, and away from possibly dying on the battlefield. Unwilling to admit he wished not to die in battle, he repressed that wish—which surfaced in his slip of the tongue and made the secondary gain of his traumatic neurosis apparent.

In short, originally his hidden wish converted into a traumatic neurosis, which saved his face and, possibly, life. But, more than likely, he had to live with psychological symptoms surfacing from repressed guilt feelings sustained by his not going back into battle.

Secondary gains, as described above, lure patients into maintaining their neurotic illnesses. Somehow, the importance of the gain, for them, far exceeds the importance of re-establishing health. It boils down to their making a deal with the devil: they escape one problem and settle for another, which puts a very low ceiling on their quality of life.

Freud also described the case of another soldier hospitalized for a traumatic war neurosis who, whenever told by his doctor or other people, "You look in really excellent form, you're certainly fit now," had an immediate attack of vomiting. Being told he was healthy, it was inferred, produced the soldier's hidden thought, "Fit and go back to service... why should I?"[6] For this patient, vomiting was a far better choice than going into battle.

The above two examples of traumatic neuroses sustained in wartime are poignant, but secondary gains can develop in any venue. Consider the following:

The Far-Reaching Effects of the Secondary Gain

In group therapy I conducted, for people with traumatic neuroses sustained in on-the-job accidents, one man suffered from multiple injuries. He always used a cane for support, but shortly after receiving a multimillion-dollar award, he no longer used it. Another member of the therapy group said, regarding the patient who stopped using a cane, "He must have gone to Lourdes," a town in France where Catholics believe Mary, the mother of Jesus, performs healing miracles.

Let's allow Otto Fenichel to take it from there: "Secondary gains may acquire the significance of one's own helplessness in order to secure external help such as was available in childhood."[7]

Therefore, some patients experience a double secondary gain: monetarily and in receiving kid-gloves treatment. Special attention may be something they missed sorely, or had too much of in childhood. Then, although suffering from disorders, they capitalize on their disabilities, and that benefit from their conditions is the secondary gain. In reaping such "rewards," they become motivated to maintain, consciously or unconsciously, their illnesses. Thus, they "luxuriate" in their suffering.

We should pay heed to Fenichel: "The question how to combat to prevent secondary gains often becomes the main problem in treatment." After 44 years of being a psychodynamic psychotherapist, it's clear to me: Protracted emotional suffering is maintained by some outright or hidden secondary gain, which adheres to the illness as if by Crazy Glue.

Many people wish to jettison their suffering but keep its hidden benefits. When such pleasure and pain become inextricably intermingled, painstaking work in therapy, with the patient's full effort, is usually the only resolution.

In short, roll up your sleeves and get to work on the above issues. They exist and won't go away by themselves. Uncover those saboteurs and send them on their way. Let us now turn to a psychological mechanism that, at the extreme, can put us out of action.

Defense

The word defense, bantered around and used loosely, is now a household term. Often we hear the statement, "He's in denial," which is a vague, informal expression and is one of many *defenses*. However, for our purposes, the *Psychiatric Dictionary* describes *defense* as a *mental mechanism that serves to protect people from the danger arising from their impulses.*[8] Why do we need such protection? Is an impulse part of the mafia? Well, that's almost the case:

An impulse is an inner sexual or aggressive desire, which seeks unmodified pleasure. But, society wants those to be modified. So, conflicts arise between the inner forces seeking unmodified pleasure and the demands of reality, between desires and restraints. Consequently, defenses develop to suppress inner desires. When the defenses are overly restrictive, or the ego is poorly developed and therefore unable to negotiate successful compromises, a neurosis can develop. We end up inhibited, sometimes immobilized. That's the worst-case scenario.

The best-case scenario: Being successful in therapy requires that patients develop trusting, open, and cooperative relationships with their therapists. *That sets the stage for therapists to help patients create a healthy internal psychological balance, to manage effectively the interplay of their powerful conflicting inner forces.* The development of a healthy inner balance is crucial to being effective with people and in life in general.

The following is an example of the consequences of an *inner imbalance*: A boss suggested to his worker that he take a human relations course necessary for his promotion. He failed to do so and was passed over. Why did this happen? Did he have a memory lapse, and consequently forget to take the course? Nope!

His low self-esteem led to his feeling unworthy, which generated an unconscious wish to fail that he acted out on. He was victimized by an internal conflict: a hidden wish to fail versus a conscious desire to succeed, and that contradiction brought him to a standstill. See more about this self-defeating mechanism in Chapter Six.

Keep in mind that defenses can be mild, moderate, or severe, and that there are different types as well. With defenses being quite complex to undo, patients should start early to identify and analyze them. In addition to patients expressing their thoughts and feelings, they need to listen carefully to what therapists have to say about their defense mechanisms. Then, they should explore those pointed out by their therapists. They can ask themselves questions: "In what circumstances did it occur?" "With whom?" In short, patients should work from every angle possible with their own insights as well as their therapists' input.

Defense mechanisms can appear in different forms: Wilhelm Reich coined the phrase *character armor*, "a compact defense mechanism against our therapeutic endeavors."[9] Anna Freud referred to, "Permanent defence [sic] phenomena…. Bodily attitudes such as stiffness and rigidity, personal peculiarities such as a fixed smile, contemptuous, ironical and arrogant behavior… that have developed into permanent character-traits."[10] "Character armor" and "permanent defense phenomena," as described above, are but two of many general descriptions of defenses. Some specific examples follow.

Basic Defense Mechanisms

Anna Freud described nine defense mechanisms, although that was in 1946. Subsequently, many more have been determined. However, the basic ones described below can be analyzed for starters; your therapist might pinpoint others:[11]

Regression: Sliding back to an earlier stage in development, for example, when a well-adjusted child no longer wants to attend school and now sucks his thumb after a newborn sibling arrives at home. Regression also occurs in adults, hence the saying, "If you fall off a horse, get back up again." Meaning, of course, don't regress, as in our prior examples of the traumatic neuroses and secondary gains.

Nowadays, we don't usually fall off horses, but we do have auto accidents and need to get back behind the steering wheel. However, in this age of disability lawsuits, we see loads of people with walkers, neck braces, slings, canes, and crutches. [Check out the award-winning *The Litigious Society* by Jethro K. Lieberman, for an eye-opening view of the extensiveness of lawsuits in our society, which is another perspective on secondary gain.]

Repression: "The withholding or expulsion of an idea or affect from the conscious ego."[12] In short, repression is a mental mechanism that blocks out a thought, feeling, or memory so the conscious mind cannot be aware of it.

Reaction Formation: The easiest way to understand this defense mechanism is by example. A person might act kind to an excessive degree, to cover over unconsciously harbored hostility.

Isolation: This defense separates feelings from their related ideas. A person might talk in a cold, detached manner about some horrific occurrence. More often, it occurs in males. For example, isolation might separate tenderness, sensitivity, and love from sex, due to faulty childhood occurrences.

Undoing: a defense often presented with its cohort, "doing," together known as "doing and undoing." One example of the latter would be washing one's hands after thinking something held to be reprehensible. The washing is an attempt to undo the objectionable thought.

Projection: If two people were to look at the same cloud, one person might say, "It looks like an angel," while the other person might say, "It seems like the devil." Each person would have projected a particular image from his or her own mind onto the cloud, stemming from each person's individual unconscious need or wish.

Introjection: In a sense, it is the opposite of projection. It is the internalizing of the image of another person, as one would like the other to be.

Turning Against the Self: This is sadism turned against the self to produce its opposite, masochism.

Reversal: Reversal, aligned closely to turning against the self, is more general in that it means shifting from one state to its opposite: when being self-destructive changes to being destructive to someone else.

Is Your Problem A Neurosis Or A Character Disorder?

This section will describe both a neurosis and a character disorder and explain the major ways patients can work optimally at freeing themselves from those psychological disorders. First, let us cover the basic nature of each.

Neurosis: A One-Stage Treatment

Neurosis is the diagnosis for a person who suffers from internal conflict, which produces anxiety, depression, and an array of psychological symptoms. In a neurosis, some people chronically obsess, "Should I follow 'Plan A' or 'Plan B?'" Finally, they assert, "I have decided not to decide." Furthermore, in most cases, a neurosis involves unresolved internal conflicts that cause distress, which increases motivation to seek help.

Generally, treatment of a neurosis is comprised of, loosely speaking, "one-stage": For example, suffering motivates some patients to rid themselves of discomfort. Since their symptoms are unacceptable to them, they avidly cooperate in treatment, and they are more apt to analyze their resistances and defenses.

Character Disorder: A Two-Stage Treatment

A character disorder, is defined as a "A pattern of behavior and emotional response ... that is socially disapproved or unacceptable with little evidence of anxiety or other symptoms seen in neuroses."[13] People with such a disorder use unacceptable interpersonal and intrapsychic strategies to avoid their internal problems.

They don't necessarily suffer from inner psychological distress: It's a *way of being* that is set, embedded, ingrained, and maladapted (according to society's standards). People with a character disorder (also known as a personality disorder) are usually not motivated to seek help from psychotherapy. That is, their ways, which are unacceptable to others, are acceptable to themselves. Often, they enjoy making a living from those unacceptable ways. Generally, their behavior bothers people around them. Their character disorders might take the form of being passive, overly aggressive, antisocial, sadistic, paranoid, or one of many other variations.

Character-disordered people are rather blasé about treatment; they insincerely accommodate their spouses, bosses, judges, or other people who have held, so to speak, guns to their heads and knives to their throats to pressure them into seeing a "shrink."

Their treatment consists of two stages. After establishing rapport, the therapist tries to pull a rabbit out of the hat. He or she attempts to help motivate those patients to change what was acceptable to them—such as malingering, distorting, lying, avoiding, and cheating—into becoming unacceptable. If successful at that, what remains is only a one-stage treatment. They now, hopefully, find their old ways to be unacceptable and get to work in attempting to change.

An In-Between Disorder: Character Neurosis

Another type of disorder—one, in a sense, in-between a character disorder and a neurosis—is termed a *character neurosis*. This concerns patients who initially present as having a neurosis, but during treatment, as the smoke clears, from the fires of anxiety or depression, character traits appear (miniature character flaws, as opposed to a total character disorder). It follows that patients with a character neurosis start out as one-stagers, which stretches into their becoming two-stagers.

Ensure's Recommendations Pertain to the Above Three Types

Almost all of *Ensure's* recommendations for patients pertain to the above three types, so the rest of this chapter will concern procedures for patients with neuroses or character problems. However, people with a character disorder or a character neurosis have a preliminary task: They must first change their own view of their character imperfections from being "acceptable" to "unacceptable," as previously explained. The following example illustrates one approach to making that change:

In therapy, the familiar strategy, "If you can't beat them, join them," is termed, "joining the defenses." By implementing that strategy, therapists make an effort to help people shift their attitudes towards their own unyielding problems.

The psychiatrist, Harold Greenwald, used that procedure in treating a psychopath, one of the worst-case scenario character disorders: they have no morals or scruples. Greenwald described how a pimp came to see him; the pimp explained how it was a good deal to have women out working for himself. Greenwald replied, "You're a jerk. I wrote a book about them [The Call Girl: A Social and Psychoanalytic Study, New York: Norton, 1958]; they made a movie out of it. I made much more money off call girls than you ever will."[14] Greenwald explained how, for a pimp, money talks, which was the only way to reach him.

People who have character disorders (or traits) don't readily change their course. Therapists try to find ways, as Greenwald attempted, to woo them away from their unacceptable behavior. The alternative: Patients do not have to wait for their therapists to join their defenses; they can do everything described in Ensure to shift their attitudes and begin making their character problems unacceptable to themselves. Taking the initiative saves time, money, and increases the odds of achieving a cure.

Generally, psychopaths (and some people with character problems as well) are failing financially, socially, emotionally, and then some. Therefore, they might consider, as in the case of Greenwald's patient, learning how to succeed from therapists, who usually do quite well in all spheres of life. Patients with character problems might explore the possibilities for handling matters more effectively in those areas in which they are deficient by learning how therapists handle similar issues.

Although therapists can't help anyone break the law, they certainly know how to negotiate the rapids of life. Just look at what they've had to cope with: hard-nosed professors; figuring out how to pass exams; becoming experts at relationships; and, succeeding at building their practices. Try talking turkey with them and see for yourself.

For example, one man came to see me for anxiety concerning a serious criminal trial he was facing. He had some anti-social features—not enough to diagnose him as an *anti-social personality disorder*—including being quite evasive and avoidant. After reviewing his history, it became clear he wasn't a dangerous person but was a bumbling individual who kept tripping over himself.

His court case wasn't going well, so I wrote an *amicus curiae* letter (friend of the court) to the judge. I explained that the patient, severely abused as a child, was not an anti-social or criminal personality. Furthermore, he unfortunately made a foolish mistake: to help a relative, he threatened someone. I added that he pursued therapy voluntarily, and, rather than have the state pay for his incarceration and treatment, the court might consider probation contingent upon his continuing therapy, for which he was paying.

Despite the judge ruling in accordance with my letter—which led the patient to be impressed by my finesse in that matter, and his wanting help also in overcoming his anxiety and in complying with probation—he always kept his appointment on Mondays but often forgot his Wednesday sessions. I explained resistance to him, which he immediately rejected by blurting out, "Naahhh, I just forgot!"

After a few more missed sessions, I took a different tact. I explained that since it wasn't resistance, he probably had *nominal aphasia,* a type of memory disorder specific to nouns, such as Wednesday, sometimes caused by brain injury. He grumbled, "Naahhh, it's resistance!" From that point on, he didn't miss appointments.

Sorry, but I can't resist another "finesse" story. A young woman, who sadly suffered from schizophrenia but was ambulatory and treatable on an outpatient basis, was in need of and eagerly sought treatment. She meritoriously cooperated in her once-per-week sessions, as best as she could, but when she left would call me half a dozen or so times. I explained in session how she needed to work with my suggestions during the week. After all, I further explained, it was undesirable for her to develop a dependency, since she actually needed to become more independent.

She appreciated what I said to her but persisted in making calls to me. My further explanations were to no avail. Finally, I tried being as kind and caring as I could while explaining that it was obvious that she needed to call me, and I held my breath, hoping not to further distress this unfortunately beleaguered woman. I then told her she could continue calling me, but I would have to charge her $15 per call. She never called again and thereafter did rather well in the treatment.

Now, why would people, who are losing out in life, not want to learn from therapists? It beats me, especially since my psychoanalyst was a master at it and willingly showed his form. I cooperated with him, tried to absorb as much as possible, and I've reaped the rewards. The point: Keep your eyes, ears, and mind open when you're working with a pro.

The Embedded Core and Character Analysis

Speaking of a master, Wilhelm Reich's book, *Character Analysis*, puts him in that very same category. Reich launches with a bold assertion: "Every neurosis is due to a conflict... [that] expresses itself in the neurotic symptom or neurotic character trait. The character represents the specific way of being of an individual, an expression of his total past..."[15]

In addition, Reich explained the treatment paradigm for character disorders: 1) pare away resistances and defenses; and 2) expose conflicts and difficulties stemming from deep within, which are referred to in *Ensure* as the *embedded core* (described more fully further on).

However, let's take Reich's approach further. The inner conflicts and problems he referred to can become agitated, inflamed, by relationship difficulties. Therefore, explore your *embedded core*. But, again, include a discussion of your relationships from your past, present, and with your therapist—comparing those, you will recall, was a technique described by Menninger and was referred to in chapters three and five. Of course, *the above does not have to be discussed all at one time*. It covers a great deal, so hold off until those issues arise spontaneously and when the timing is right.

Reich's principles, coupled with Menninger's, can help to free you from your emotional problems, be they a neurosis or character disorder. View those as an important aspect of your work in therapy, which does not mean you have to talk only about the aforementioned. Talk about everything, free associate, but remember Reich's and Menninger's proposals.

I'm not suggesting you memorize those or any of *Ensures* principles, but you can keep them in mind. That is, in traveling by auto from New York to Canada, of course you would pay heed to the countless towns, villages, cities, and states you encountered, yet all the while being aware, somehow, somewhere in your mind, that you are heading north. Keep the embedded core and your relationships in that very same "somehow, somewhere" place in your mind.

Again, the embedded core, comprised of conflicts, repressed issues, and other matters, which psychotherapists emphasize as being an inner source of psychological disturbance, is at the root of neuroses and character disorders. Consequently, it is of dire importance to look at the overbearing impact of all sorts of negative early childhood influences from diverse perspectives.

The task might seem daunting, but it is not. It requires patience during the process of slowly, steadily, and readily free associating— merely saying whatever passes through your mind, no words barred, session after session. Eventually, patients unravel their defenses, effectively laying the groundwork for their cures.

Remember, Reich referred to "character armor," the totality of character traits resulting in a compact of defense mechanisms against therapeutic efforts. The solution: be forewarned and forearmed. Look for openings and tease the armor apart, with words, thoughts, feelings, and associations.

Additional Clues to Undoing Character Armor

When you find openings in your armor realize that opportunity knocks. Free-associate to those gifts: dreams, slips, errors, your attitude, your manner of saying things, how you are silent (defiant, passive, stubborn, tense…). Some people say that a man can determine just how a woman feels toward him simply by listening to how she says his name (and vice versa).

Don't wait for your therapist to point out your peccadilloes. Be open to perceiving and analyzing those. Doing so will help you abandon heavy burdens. Some concrete examples: *pressure of speech,* which consists of a person not letting another get a word in edgewise, is a severe control mechanism; *harshness or screeching* when talking, distorts one's emotions; *stiff or clunky movements or posture,* are manifestations of character armor. Once again, heed the words of Reich: "The character resistance expresses itself not in the content of the material, but in the formal aspects of the general behavior, the manner of talking, of the gait, facial expression and typical attitudes such as smiling, deriding, haughtiness, overcorrectness, the manner of the politeness or of the aggression, etc."[16]

We Are Overly Adapted

Our sensory nerve endings report to us what goes on in the world around—that's one of our survival mechanisms. But, if any particular nerve ending is overly stimulated, it stops transmitting messages—known as *sensory adaptation*—to prevent our brains from being flooded with information.

Similarly, our systems also tune out physical and emotional feelings, thoughts, memories, wishes, fantasies, dreams, and so on. Unfortunately, we can become so shut down that at an extreme we have the *depersonalization* syndrome, in which people feel they have lost their personal identities. What goes along for the ride is *derealization,* a part of depersonalization, in which people also feel that they are in a strange or unreal environment. They become dejected, apathetic, bewildered, or feel emotionally empty; they find difficulty in organizing, collecting, and arranging thoughts; their heads feel numb and their brains feel deadened.[17]

I hope you're happy, not dejected, and that your brain is scintillating, not deadened. But, if you have any of that shutdown stuff, open up to your therapist concerning everything about yourself. She knows what to do with it all. Get out of the shutdown mode, which you'll discover how to do in the very next chapter.

REFERENCES – FIVE

1. Sigmund Freud, "Those Wrecked By Success," *The Standard Edition,* Vol. 16, pp. 286-287.
2. Jonathan Shedler, (2010). "The Efficacy of Psychodynamic Psychotherapy," *American Psychologist,* Vol. 65, No. 2, 98-109.
3. Norman Doidge, *The Brain That Changes Itself* (New York: Penguin Books, 2007).
4. "Taxi Drivers' Brains 'Grow' on the Job," BBC News World Edition, March 14, 2000, 1, http://www.news.bbc.co.uk/2/hi/677048.stm.
5. Sigmund Freud, *The Complete Works* (London: Hogarth Press, 1926/1953), XX, pp. 223-224.
6. Ibid., VI, pp. 114-115.
7. Otto Fenichel, *The Psychoanalytic Theory of Neurosis* (New York: W. W. Norton, 1945), pp. 126-127.
8. Robert J. Campbell, *Psychiatric Dictionary,* 6th ed. (New York: Oxford University Press, 1989), p. 174.
9. Wilhelm Reich, *Character Analysis* (New York: Farrar, Straus & Giraux, 1968/1933), p. 44.
10. A. Freud, p. 35.
11. Ibid., p. 47.
12. Ibid., p. 55.
13. *Blakiston's Pocket Medical Dictionary,* 4th ed. (New York: McGraw Hill Book Company, 1979), p. 154.
14. Harold Greenwald, "Treatment of the Psychopath," in *Active Psychotherapy,* ed. by Harold Greenwald (New York: Jason Aronson, 1967), p. 371.
15. Wilhelm Reich, *Character Analysis* (New York: The Noonday Press, 1949), p. 3-4.
16. Ibid., p. 45.
17. Robert J. Campbell, *Psychiatric Dictionary* (New York: Oxford University Press, 1989), p. 191.

SIX

Become Free from Your "Embedded Core"

THE TOTAL BODY of ideas and experiences unique to each of us, which is complex and runs deep, is referred to as the *apperception mass*. Freud used a closely related phrase, *the deep inner needs of our nature,* in advising Theodore Reik regarding his career and pending marriage.... "When making a decision of minor importance, I have always found it advantageous to consider all the pros and cons. In vital matters, however, such as the choice of a mate or a profession, the decision should come from the unconscious, from the deep inner needs of our nature."[1]

So, all's well if our apperception mass, or deep inner needs of our nature, is well. However, if an embedded core of flaws exists, it might lead us to be ineffective in relationships, making decisions, and then some. Before we can make proper decisions arising from our apperception mass, or the deep inner needs of our nature, we need to undo our embedded core, more fully described below. That core, again, consists of hidden flaws, repressed issues, conflicts, and other factors, which are our inner source of psychological disturbance and are at the root of neuroses and character disorders.

Hidden Flaws: Drawing A Conclusion from A Minor Characteristic

The world-renowned psychiatrist Silvano Arieti provided us with a vivid but extreme example of one flaw in thinking and handling emotions, which can wreak havoc. Arieti explained that a patient of his thought she was the Virgin Mary because "The Virgin Mary was a virgin; I am a virgin; therefore I am the Virgin Mary...."[2]

Arieti's patient concluded that she was the Virgin Mary, because they were both virgins. However, the commonality of their virginity is a *minor characteristic,* from which conclusions are not drawn—to do so comprises a serious flaw in thinking.

According to logic, we draw conclusions based on the similarity of a *major characteristic:* Therefore, only the woman who gave birth to Jesus Christ was *the* Virgin Mary, and Arieti's patient was indeed a different person.

The following is a more commonly occurring example of the above flaw—namely, drawing a conclusion from a minor characteristic: Joe, a psychopath, told Sharon he loves her. Sharon, although a regular person, is desperate. Despite knowing Joe is a psychopath, she affirmed her love for him. And so, they plan to get married.

However, their major characteristics don't jibe: He is a psychopath; she is "a regular person." Therefore, in this case, "love" is a minor factor.

Sharon's desperation produced emotional blindness. But Joe is not blind: to the contrary, he sees rather well. His eyes are riveted on a "live one on his hook." Hence the saying, "When you kiss a thief, hold onto your wallet." Sharon should not walk down the aisle with Joe, but she should immediately run for the hills.

The Basic Fault

Michael Balint, in *The Doctor, His Patient and the Illness* (1957), described another flaw. He discovered that some patients felt something was not psychologically right, that something was missing in their emotional makeup, which he termed the *basic fault.* From childhood on, they compensated by making artificial adjustments that altered their natural way of being.

The basic fault in my own personal case: I felt tainted by my father's suicide. *My artificial adjustment*: I would freeze in anticipation of someone making that bleak discovery. *What's remarkable*: I've been free from that blemish for so many years, thanks to psychotherapy. *What can follow*: Just about anyone who makes a good adjustment to psychotherapy can overcome just about any flaw.

The Pursuit of Failure and the Idealization of Unhappiness[3]

Roy Schafer explained that many people who expect too much from themselves and always fall short, have an unconscious need for self-destructiveness; and they "sexualize suffering."[4] For one possible example, some people claim that, "Sex is great after we fight and then make up." For those people, since suffering is connected to pleasure, they maintain that pattern rather than analyzing and resolving their disturbances.

According to Schafer, people who "always fall short" and "sexualize suffering," suffer emotionally and are unable to succeed; unconsciously, they *pursue failure and idealize unhappiness*. In Schafer's own words, "Those people who suffer from repetitive failure and chronic unhappiness present themselves as afflicted or as victimized, but their failures prove to have been pursued. Similarly, the unhappiness frequently proves to have been self-inflicted."[5]

In therapy, those sufferers avoid getting well and are ingenious at finding ways to fail. And, they talk about how unhappy they are but in ways indicating they idealize that state. Again and according to Schafer, they unconsciously pursue failure and idealize unhappiness.

In summary, the above inner flaws exist within some people, in varying degrees and types, and form an inner composite, referred to in *Ensure,* as an *embedded core.* The latter leads to neuroses, character disorders, psychosomatic illnesses, and then some. However, feelings of inferiority (Adler), repressed thoughts, wishes, or feelings (Freud), impact from neglect (Spitz), and many other factors as well, can be part of the mix.

And that is the point: A *mix of inner factors, unique to each person*, needs to be addressed in the course of therapy. It's probably best to avoid looking for one or the other flaws; instead, express what you have uncovered as you explore. One person's feeling of having been rejected, might surface as another's feeling inferior. But, rather than use psychological terms, as I have here or there, describe your inner life through natural expressions, according to how you experienced those events or circumstances.

For example, once again, here's how Kafka put it, concerning his father: "That's why I could show my thanks to you for everything only as a beggar does…" And, in my case, described in *Ensure's* Introduction, recall how I related the beating given to me: "Without warning, he started swinging. Frightened, I thought, 'One more smack and that's what death is.'" Uncover, uproot, and unravel whatever is in your guts eating away at you, once and for all, by saying it the way it is.

How Flaws Develop

Negative Experiences

Some children encounter faulty, abusive, traumatic, sneglectful, or ill-conceived experiences that negatively affect their developing minds and ultimately their lives as adults. If you wore eyeglasses tinted gray, everything would look gray. Similarly, negative experiences sustained in childhood taint our perception as adults.

Perhaps a more vivid analogy is that some people's early negative experiences seem to form a template, which they overlay onto other people or situations. The targets then take on the negative characteristics carved into the template. So, someone terrorized on a cold, snowy day can feel terrorized years later on a day with similar weather, whereas others joyously anticipate going sledding. As a child, while I was sitting at my desk studying, my father brutally smacked me, and for years afterward, I had anxiety while studying. Nowadays, studying, researching, and learning are joyous for me (thanks to psychotherapy).

Often, many people don't consciously feel they were terrorized, even if that were the case in childhood. More than likely, as Balint described, they have made artificial adjustments that skirt their inner feeling of being terrorized or flawed. For example, a family might casually be eating dinner together, yet one of them, previously abused, might camouflage the terror existing within his embedded core, through artificial adjustments, such as overeating, restlessness...

Children and adults don't do well in emotionally empty relationships. Infants suffer, deteriorate, or in fact even die, depending on the degree of deprivation they experience. The following information clearly indicates the importance for people in therapy to understand and explore from whence they came, namely, what their childhood was like:

Deprivation

A paper I published in 2014, was partly based on FBI statistics for the year 2010. It held that *emotional deprivation* in the age range under 10 was the precursor for the conduct, psychopath, and criminal disorders.[6] That inference was based on the fact that studies from developmental psychology and psychiatry jibed with the FBI's statistics.[7] The highlights from those studies will follow after the FBI's data shown below:

- 10,223,558 arrests for violent and non-violent crimes in 2010.
- age range under ten... 8,205
- age range 10-14... 341,490
- age range 15-19... 1,906,693
- age range 20-24... 2,046,577

That extraordinary progression led me to infer that the conduct, psychopath, and criminal disorders germinated in infancy due to emotional deprivation. Then, those disorders erupted and increased enormously throughout the teenage and early adult years. And, providing further confirmation of the above inference, is the statistic that "Between 65 percent and 70 percent of the children and adolescents arrested each year have a mental health disorder."[8]

To be sure, many of the adults who suffer from *minor*, not *severe*, abuse in childhood nevertheless suffer from a basic fault or flaw. Should you fit *anywhere* on the continuum from minor to severe abuse occurring at any age, face the facts, discuss them with your therapist, so he or she can help you find ways to help you unburden yourself.

Far too many people have an aversion to confronting such unpleasantries, whether those are minor or severe, and avoid doing so initially in treatment. However, if that's your plight, not to worry: in time, through analysis of resistance, facing your problems straightaway will become palatable.

Be Free from Psychological Problems Set in Childhood

Some History

For some perspective on the importance of addressing your childhood in your therapy, consider the following:

- Two thousand years ago, Sophocles made it clear, particularly in his play Oedipus Rex, that the ancient Greeks believed psychological disorders were set in childhood.
- In the 1890s, Freud began to formalize that concept.
- In 1933, Reich emphasized focusing on repression that occurs in childhood.
- In 1938, Menninger pointed to the triangle for patients to explore, as we referred to earlier, and one corner of it is early childhood.
- And, in 2010, as previously referred to, Shedler asserted, "The goal of psychoanalytic psychotherapy is to loosen the bonds of past experience [childhood] to create new life possibilities."

Sophocles, Freud, Menninger, Reich, Shedler... They are telling us something: "Explore your childhood experiences." Consider that something is pushing up your symptoms (most likely, your core of embedded issues) and driving you to consider or already be in therapy. Either way, you should recognize the importance of looking into your childhood history.

It is part of human nature to push aside negative occurrences in childhood, sort of hoping they'll fade away. But, in therapy you can overcome their destructive influence by merely talking about them.

In that spirit, the following plights in childhood that are cited, are presented to help stir you to look into your own childhood, and explore it in therapy. Consequently, you can relieve yourself of any of your childhood's detrimental effects.

To Achieve a Cure, Explore Your Childhood

Our minds and emotions start forming early in infancy. A good indicator of the first signs of the mind developing is the infant's smile upon recognizing its mother. The following is a vivid description of the mother-infant scenario depicted by Althea Horner, an expert in child development: "Breastfeeding is no guarantee of an optimal mother-infant relationship; [if there are] ... subtle attitudes of interest and disinterest, there will be a variation in the quality of mother-infant interaction from the start. The optimal attitude ... 'primary maternal preoccupation' ... is a state of heightened sensitivity of the mother toward the infant, which brings her into smooth and harmonious interaction with her baby."[9]

Attachment: Always Loving and Attentive

Horner refers to the primary maternal nurturance of the infant as *attachment*, which means that a mother (or other caretaker) always stays on a loving and attentive course with her infant. A mother (the object) must therefore always be involved (constant), or *attached*, as it were. Horner cites Anna Freud's statement that "Object constancy means... to retain attachment even when the person is unsatisfying."[10] Attachment enables the infant to be spoon-fed social learning.

Alas, many of us lacked such complete love and attention early on, so now it's a do it yourself job. In therapy, consider what went right or wrong for you, as far back as you can remember. But don't be bogged down by judging yourself, your parents, or anyone else. Just explore its impact on you and find ways to let go of negative influences: Open yourself up to new and positive relationships. Assimilate the good feelings derived from those.

How the Embedded Core Starts in Infancy

The following studies and statistics, while they might not pertain to what happened to you in childhood or infancy, nevertheless illustrate how the embedded core reaches into the earliest stages.

First, don't be alarmed by possibly thinking, "Well, there is no hope for me then. It's not possible to remember things from early childhood or infancy, so I would not be able to discuss them, even if they actually took place." Fortunately, Freud discovered a process that helps patients retrieve memories. It's a powerful and therapeutic way of recalling "lost" memories through analysis of transference, discussed throughout *Ensure* but more fully in Chapter Seven. So, tolerate that dark uncertainty about your childhood a bit longer, until you read that chapter, and discover how to shine a bright light upon your early memories to provide further relief for yourself in therapy.

Now, some grim facts about strife in childhood: Whether those are similar to your situation or not, they are presented in the hope of motivating you to look into your own history. But just knowing about exploring the possible oppression or deficits you might have sustained is not enough. To feel the relief, explore and then implement the full scope of analysis: Doing so will provide major benefits.

Some FBI and U.S. Government Data: Children and Infants' Maltreatment

In 2011, 9.9 children per 1,000 suffered from maltreatment. They also faced housing problems, injury, mortality, and alcohol and illicit drug use.[11] Younger children are more frequently victims of child maltreatment than older children. In 2011, there were 23 maltreatment reports per 1,000 children under age 1.[12] Cases of maltreatment in 2011 decreased as children advanced beyond age 1. The FBI also reported that children 2 and 3 years of age (!) were involved in setting fires, but the mean age ranged from 9 to 12.[13]

In short, the above data points to the considerable amount of infant and child maltreatment. We will consider some other vantage points regarding this problem and then consider its relevance to people in therapy.

Psychiatric Studies of Infants Deprived of Their Mothers' Nurturance

René Spitz's classic research makes the importance of a mother's love and attention undeniable. He showed that infants were impaired when deprived of a significant quantity or quality of their mothers' nurturance (attachment). In 1952, he filmed infants in their cribs, deprived of their mothers or adequate substitutes for months, in their first year or so of life.[14] Spitz describes, and it is vividly apparent, how their "development becomes retarded in the course of the first two months of separation.... [Each child] becomes increasingly unapproachable, weepy and screaming." Spitz referred to this as *anaclitic depression*.

He also reported that infant withdrawal becomes complete after three months of separation; after five months, they "deteriorate progressively," becoming "lethargic, their motility retarded, their weight and growth arrested.... Their faces become vacuous... activity is restricted to atypical... finger movements. They are unable to sit, stand, walk or talk."

Spitz concluded that the *quality* of the mother-child relationship can be a precursor to the development of *psychosomatic illnesses*. However, *the lack of time spent* in the mother-child relationship correlates to the development of *emotional deficiency*. "This classification offers viewpoints that were found useful both in therapy and in preventive psychiatry."

Additional FBI statistics reveal some unpalatable facts about how damaging early negative influences are on children. From 2000 to 2004, in schools alone, 12 children were arrested, who were 4-years old or less, as well as 2,028 in the age range of 5-9.[15] Hurt, failure, and sundry other negative childhood experiences can instill unconscious, destructive needs.

The consequences of the mishandling of infants and children are dire. Damages laid down in those tender years don't just evaporate. They persist. Set your mind to overcoming any such misfortunes, rather than continuing to cover them over. The following section shows how the effects described above can linger and surface from a mild to a disastrous degree:

A Progressive Continuum: Self-defeating... Self-destructive... Chronic Suicide... Acute Suicide

Impulses and trends that fall anywhere in the above continuum can begin as early as infancy. If untreated, they lay the foundation for defensiveness. If allowed to persist, they can ruin chances for success or become malignant and advance to the point of suicide. Heed the words of Karl Menninger who describes the difference between chronic and acute suicide:

> In the former the individual postpones death indefinitely, at a cost of suffering and impairment of function which is equivalent to a partial suicide—a 'living death,' is true, but is nevertheless living. In such persons, however, the destructive urge is often of a progressive nature, requiring larger and larger payments until finally the individual is, as it were, bankrupted and must surrender to actual death.[16]

Please keep in mind that I have pointed out the four levels on the continuum, because each has a calamitous potential with roots in the embedded core. Each is capable of flaring up and causing disastrous consequences. It's no wonder that suicide is one of the ten leading causes of death in the U.S.[17] In 2014, there were 42,773 deaths from suicide in the U.S., a 24% increase from 1999.[18]

Further on we will address opening up a pathway through therapy to overcoming the above potentially disastrous patterns. However, if you're still skeptical about destructive tendencies forming in infancy, the following eye-opening research certainly should persuade you:

Multiple Self-Destructive Attempts by Children Age Range 2 ½ to 5

The Child Outpatient Clinic of the University of Massachusetts Medical Center in Worcester evaluated 16 children in the age range 2 1/2 to 5 after they seriously injured themselves. Thirteen of those children made multiple self-destructive attempts, such as deliberately setting themselves on fire, ingesting drugs, jumping from high places, cutting or stabbing themselves, darting out into speeding traffic, trying to drown themselves, banging their heads with lethal intent, or throwing themselves down stairs. They manifested symptoms of depression. In addition, they were victims of child abuse, neglect, and were largely unwanted.[19]

Some of those children saw death as reversible; after either suicide attempts or bona fide accidents, they showed no pain and didn't cry when injured. Their craving for affection and love, it seems, had become twisted into desperate, self-destructive mechanisms—frozen into their psyches—that demanded attention and sympathy.

Accordingly, children afflicted with that pattern carry it forward into adulthood. It crops up in the forms of fear of success, the pursuit of failure, the idealization of unhappiness... Even if they attain success, under those arduous conditions, the fulfillment of the sufferers' self-destructive wishes wrecks them. Buried deep within their inner psyche is a contorted concept of what elicits love; it manifests itself in suffering (masochism).

And, as Menninger described, such ruinous patterns can progress to actual suicide in adulthood. Unconscious self-destructive wishes and behaviors are engendered by abuse, rejection, or abandonment in infancy.

Consider the case of my father, described in *Ensure's* Introduction. He was, as you will recall, an orphan before age six, which, in addition to other complications, must have caused him to suffer from terrible deprivation early on. The effects of that early trauma led to his developing a *manic depressive* disorder—nowadays known as *bipolar*. That condition worsened when his business failed, resulting in his suicide.

If he sought help to address and overcome the effects of childhood trauma, his life might have been spared. His is just one example of tens of thousands of cases of suicide that occur annually, which start with a history of disastrous childhoods. To a lesser degree, millions of people with less noxious histories maintain lifetime patterns of being self-defeating or self-destructive, or they persist with a chronic suicide disposition. Make certain you're not on that list.

Recognize, Explore, Analyze, and Resolve Subtle Clues before They Become Malignant

Childish, more accurately infantile, behavior and thought patterns—pouting, helplessness, self-inflicted pain, sexual inhibitions or anomalies, giving up, tantrums, complaining—carry forward and ensnare some adults tighter than a straitjacket. They can't emerge from their emotional restraints. Although consciously they pursue success, unconsciously they are stalking failure, precluding their attaining, maintaining, or enjoying their accomplishments.

Freedom from Self-Directed Destructiveness

The above-detailed clues too frequently are ignored; but, when failure strikes, dejection grabs the victim's attention. Become aware and wary of subtle clues. Realize you are making a decision to ignore those; that is a decision, which can be reversed by recognizing, exploring, analyzing, and resolving self-directed destructive thoughts, feelings, and behavior.

Take the information garnered from *Ensure* and use it as an aid to freeing yourself—by participating effectively in psychotherapy—from debilitating flaws that have roots in childhood. It may take time. But, in all honesty, can you think of any worthier cause?

A Major Step: Emotional Separation and Individuation

One major aspect of progressing from an infant to a healthy adult involves being able to, literally and figuratively, stand on your own two feet, a succinct metaphor for the highly complex process of human development. Essentially, newborn infants function biologically. Their behavior is determined solely by biological factors, namely, chemical, anatomical, and physiological ones. However, adults are *psychobiological*: When fully developed, their minds, in conjunction with biological factors, can direct their behavior.

What constitutes being fully developed? The entire study of developmental psychology seeks to answer that question. For our purposes, it begins with becoming emotionally free from dependent ties to parents (separation) and becoming a unique individual (individuated). Developing freedom from dependency and being your own person is a complex process, which Margaret S. Mahler described as *separation and individuation*.[20] As an adult, loosening the bonds to past experience is the precursor to undergoing that process.

In undoing emotional ties in order to become emotionally free, of course, does not mean one stops loving or having a relationship with parents, and the same pertains to becoming independent. It means letting go, undoing, through therapy, detrimental influences that may have accrued in your childhood. Namely, feelings of rejection; dependency; the need to suffer; intolerance for success... in short, any and all, sources of the characteristics on the continuum of self-defeating... self-destructive... chronic suicide... and especially, any shred, remnant, hint, or trace of actual suicide. In the positive terms put forth by Abraham Maslow, it means becoming a fully functioning person.

REFERENCES - SIX

1. Theodor Reik, *Listening With The Third Ear* (New York: Pyramid Publications, 1948), p.7.
2. Silvano Arieti, *Interpretation of Schizophrenia* (New York: Basic Books, 1974), p. 231.
3. Roy Schafer, "The Pursuit of Failure and the Idealization of Unhappiness," *American Psychologist*, 1984, Vol.39, 398.
4. Ibid., pp. 398-405.
5. Ibid., p. 398.
6. Ira Schwartz, "Conduct Disorders, Psychopaths, and Criminals Begone! Society Can Prevail!" *American Journal of Forensic Psychology*, 2014, Vol. 32, 3, pp. 5-9.
7. Federal Bureau of Investigation: Crime in the United States, 2012. Lanham, MD, Bernan Press, 2012, pp. 341-342.
8. National Conference of State Legislators. Juvenile Justice Guide Book for Legislators, November 10, 2011; 2. http://www.models-forchange.net/uploads/ cms/documents/ jjguidebook-mental.pdf
9. Althea J. Horner, *Object Relations and the Developing Ego in Therapy*. New York, Jason Aronson, 1979, p. 43.
10. Ibid., p. 35.
11. Federal Interagency Forum on Child and Family Statistics: America's Children: Key National Indicators of Well Being, 2013. Washington, DC, U.S. Government Printing Office/National Center for Health Statistics, July 2013, p. 29.
12. Ibid., p. 11.
13. U.S. Department of Justice, Federal Bureau of Investigation, Law Enforcement Communication Unit, Training and Development Division: Juvenile arson. FBI Law Enforcement Bulletin, April 2005; 74:4:3.
14. Rene A. Spitz, Emotional "Deprivation in Infancy: study by René A. Spitz. 1952. http://www.youtube.com/watch?v=VvdOe10vrs4.
15. U.S. Department of Justice, Federal Bureau of Investigation, Criminal Justice Information Services Division, Crime Analysis,

Research and Development Unit: Crime in Schools and Colleges: A Study of Offenders and Arrestees Reported via National Incident-Based Reporting System Data, October 2007; 17. http://www.fbi.gov/about-us/cjis/ucr/nibrs/crime-in-schools-and-colleges-pdf.

16. Karl A. Menninger, *Man Against Himself,* New York, Harcourt, Brace and Company, 1938, pp. 88-9.

17. Centers for Disease Control and Prevention, http://www.cdc.gov/nchs/fastats/leading-causes-of-death.htm.

18. Centers for Disease Control and Prevention, http://www.cdc.gov/nchs/databriefs/db241.htm.

19. P.A. Rosenthal and S. Rosenthal, "Suicidal Behavior by Preschool Children," *The American Journal of Psychiatry,* 1984, 141, 4.

20. Margaret S. Mahler, *The Selected Papers of Margaret S. Mahler: Vol. Two, Separation-Individuation,* published by Jason Aronson (1979)

SEVEN

You and Your Therapist

Using Your Therapist as a Guide

AS YOUR THERAPIST says things to you, consider what she says to be droplets of helpful feedback that, over time, will add up and serve you well. The atmosphere therapists create is comprised mainly of empathy and helpful things they say, to be expanded on later in this chapter. That ambiance will help you grow if you are mentally active in sessions. Being active in sessions should lead to some easing of distress; you'll then be able to take new and effective actions, based on what you have taken from your therapist and your own insights, leading to further progress.

For example, when you first learned how to ride a bicycle or swim, you struggled, but eventually it clicked—you got going. Then, regardless of some wavering, you maintained momentum. In similar fashion, your therapist's comments will add up and you'll gain impetus, providing you work with her input: In and out of sessions, *activate what you've taken from your sessions.*

That process will stimulate your gaining insights. Verbalize the insights, even if they are incomplete, but don't misconstrue those to be permanent, carved in stone. In therapy, as you overcome suffering and other problems, your desired way of being will develop slowly, so what you uncover about yourself today will put you in a position to become different tomorrow, as you carefully move toward your goals. Let mutability reign supreme; change is what you're seeking and undergoing. You're in the process of becoming...

Described below are some of the things therapists do that are salutary. Become aware of them, and then see them in action in your sessions. Participate constructively to your therapist's input; be open to considering the things your therapist describes about you, which includes his referring to your strengths.

Although we are about to describe what therapists do, which clearly implies the importance of at least considering whatever they say, please keep the following in mind: *Patients should express spontaneously whatever they sense or feel without necessarily waiting for their therapists to infer or suggest something the patient "might be experiencing." According to many therapists, a patient's own discovery and expression of a thought, feeling, or motive, of which previously they were unaware, is of the utmost importance.*

Tuning Into Your Therapist

Let yourself become accustomed to the unique therapeutic ambiance. Start to enjoy the freedom it provides for you, by letting your guard down in that safe environment. Learn to benefit from the climate of "unconditional positive regard," as Carl Rogers described it, custom made for you by your therapist.

What Do Therapists Do?

Become familiar with the ways, in general, that therapists participate in the therapy process. It is a given that therapists listen carefully and relate in an easygoing manner to help patients adjust and feel comfortable. However, they also contribute in other important ways, and your awareness of those should help maximize your benefits. Therefore, consider the following:

Therapists...

establish rapport by fostering mutual confidence and understanding between their patients and themselves. They establish teamwork and a working alliance.

provide empathy, considered by many to be the core of the therapeutic relationship. It consists of therapists seeing patients' situations as if those were his or her own. They "stand in patients' shoes," so to speak.

clarify by encouraging discussions about what patients and they have said, in order to derive at mutual understandings.

confront, that is, they listen and then point out issues that might be beneficial for the patient to talk about—perhaps addressing contradictions, inconsistencies, or things noteworthy in what patients have said.

interpret, meaning they explain what seems to be unconsciously causing patients' symptoms, and they analyze the way patients relate to their therapists. That latter analysis helps free patients from their psychological problems—described previously as analysis of the transference.

reconstruct through inferences drawn from information provided by the patient. Therapists sometimes offer educated guesses. That is, they surmise what might have happened in the past to stimulate their patients' recollections.

help set the stage for working through those issues that arise, such as something an interpretation has revealed or explained. Therapists and patients must repeatedly work together on those issues over time. That process is critical for progress in treatment.

are vigilant about helping patients analyze their resistances and defenses, a process that paves the way for patients to release their inner naturalness.

The Ultimate Process to Ensure Your Cure

The ultimate instrument on the way to achieving a cure in psychodynamic psychotherapy is the *mutative interpretation*. It is the total effect of the many, many explanations (interpretations) provided by your therapist as to why you feel anxious, obsessed, depressed... If you have been open to working positively with those interpretations, they form a composite that creates a rift in your neurosis or character disorder, enabling your natural, healthy functioning to emerge.

By using the information from *Ensure* in your therapy, you will pave the way for the mutative interpretation to occur. That intervention by therapists has always been the bulwark of therapy, providing patients cooperate. That is, its effectiveness depends on patients working constructively with what therapists put forth to them. The mutative interpretation was Freud's innovation; its ultimate importance still prevails.

However, many innovators have added other dimensions to gaining a cure, some described in *Ensure,* which have increased the scope of the curative force:

Anna Freud, expanded her father's techniques, by emphasizing the analysis of defenses, which she described in her book, *The Ego and the Mechanisms of Defence* (1946) International Universities Press, NY. She considered the defensive operations as an object of analysis.

Her work opened up the development of a focus on the ego's capacity, in and of itself, to grow and develop. That is, with defenses removed, a person's ego is capable of growth and development. In short, we are capable of developing, if we remove defenses and then become active in new ways.

In addition, other theorists began to emphasize the importance of analyzing patients' relationships. Consequently, interpersonal relations and the nature of one's own self grew in importance.

Your therapist's particular style will be composed of some of the approaches described in *Ensure*. Of course, many other variations exist. However, what you have read about in *Ensure* are mainstays of therapy: namely, reflecting; free associating; analyzing resistance; loosening bonds to past experience; opening up new pathways prescribed by you; and more. Those factors you've taken from *Ensure* should help you develop a cooperative therapeutic attitude, which will be of ultimate importance in your therapy.

Consider as an analogy, the functioning of an orchestra. The maestro leads and synchronizes the different sounds made by violins, drums, trombones, and many other instruments, and the musicians must respond in accordance with their leader, to create harmony. Likewise, use *Ensure's* information to help you synchronize with your leader, your maestro—your therapist—and create harmony in your life by achieving your cure in psychotherapy.

Appendix A

The Typed and Unabridged Letter from Dr. Ira Schwartz' Father

Dear Ira was very glad to hear from you I think you that you care for me better ┼than the rest of family outside of Mother & Lillian [my oldest sister; I am the youngest of five siblings] as they have written but the rest well they are all Big sh ts Well to prove to you that a-I appreciate the letter you have written whatever bad you have done since I went away I will forget, But Lord pitty you if you make any wrong moves from now on.

Well my trip was perfectly normal outside of Flying between New Felind & Ire-Ierland was very cold as we were flying 20,000 ft above sea level & I mean cold. You akh-ask me about Italy Well they are very Poor country little boys & girls walk around Barefooted Now meaning winter time like you do with shoes on. You cannot by coal or wood there it is very dear so we when they get a little paper they build fire & warm Their feet little Boys go out begging for food. I know a lot of-people that I have met Through business but after hrs I don't have Nobody to talk to as I cannot talk their language in business hrs I have an interpreter.

Rome was not bombed at all but I drove in Taxi from Naples to about 150 miles Rome along water front & there are very few building left.

Spoke to Chaufer as best as I could & asked if Americans Make good job with Boom Boom. He said oh yes good Boom Boom you don't have to worry much about anything in Italy in fact all Europe all you have to say is American & they crap in their pants but they try to cheat you. The Hotel I was stopping in Rome very High Class but could not eat there as they were only feeding Unra guests Leo will explain to you who Unra is I made trip in 20 hours to Rome. You say you wish you were here well it is a big change but remember there is only one U.S.A. especially for Americans ~~oo~~ and Biggest of all is our family. I did not do any business in Italy as yet but I will and & I will make arrangements before I get through that you & Donald & Wallace [Leo's sons] & rest of my boys will have something to look forward to if you are smart enough. you say you are at a loss for words well I don't think that you have Missed anything. I do hope that you don't give Mother & Janice [my sister] no trouble & I am sure you will be alright & I will try & get home soon. Give My regard to all

Your Dad

Appendix B

A Photocopy of the Handwritten Letter from Dr. Ira Schwartz' Father

X-CEL Shoe & Clothing Co., Inc.

CABLE ADDRESS
"EXELSHOE - NEW YORK"

123 WILLIAM STREET • NEW YORK 7, N. Y. • CORTLANDT 7-1823-4-5

BUREAUX A BRUXELLES
HOTEL ALBERT 1er
BRUXELLES (Gare du Nord)
CHAMBRE 117
TÉLÉPHONE 17.22.50
ADRESSE TÉLÉGRAPHIQUE
EXELSHOE BRUXELLES

spoke to chaufer as best as I could &
asked him if americans make good
job with Boom Boom he said
oh yes good Boon Boon you dont
have to worry much about anything in Italy
in fact all Europe all you have to say is
american + they crap in their pants wail they
try to cheat you. The hotel I was stopping in Rome
very Hi gu class but could not eat there as they
were only feeding Unra, guests Leo will explain
to you who Unra is I made trip in 20 hours
to Rome. You say you wish you were here
well it is a vry change but remember
there is only one U.S.A. specially for americans
oo and Biggest of all is our family. I did not
do any business in Italy as yet but I will
+ I will make arrangments before I go through
that you Donald + Wallace + rest of my boys
will have something to look forward to if
yours are smart enough. you say you are at
a loss for words well I dont think that you
have missed anything, I do hope that you dont
give Mothers + Janie no trouble + I am sure you
will be alright + I will try + get home soon. Give
my regard to all   your dad.

Index

CPSIA information can be obtained
at www.ICGtesting.com
Printed in the USA
LVOW10s2330050517

533474LV00001B/116/P

9 781478 762775